G000144924

LEARNING
— TO —
BEHAVE

Kogan Page Books for Teachers series
Series Editor: Tom Marjoram

LEARNING
— TO —
BEHAVE

Curriculum and Whole School
Management Approaches to Discipline

EDITED BY

NEVILLE JONES & EILEEN BAGLIN JONES

KOGAN
PAGE

To Bruce and Louise

First published in 1992

Kogan Page Limited
120 Pentonville Road
London N1 9JN

© Neville Jones, Eileen Baglin Jones and named contributors, 1992

British Library Cataloguing in Publication Data
A CIP record for this book is available from the British Library.

ISBN 0 7494 0821 9

Typeset by Witwell Ltd, Southport
Printed and bound in Great Britain by Biddles Ltd,
Guildford and Kings Lynn

Contents

Notes on Contributors

Nigel Blagg is a senior educational psychologist currently seconded from his normal LEA duties to lead the development of the Somerset Thinking Skills Course. He is author of *School Phobia and Its Treatment* (1987) and published *Can We Teach Intelligence?* (1990).

Michael Boulton has been Advisor on the Medical Research Council-funded project 'Family Background Factors Characteristic of Victims and Bullies in Middle Childhood' since 1990. He has published extensively on matters relating to child development especially in relation to pupil play, aggression and bullying.

David Bowdler is an Area Educational Psychologist with the Service Children's Education Authority in Germany. He has published on such issues as non-school attendance, goal planning, and Somerset Thinking Skills.

Helen Cowie trained as a psychologist, teacher and psychotherapist, and is at present a senior lecturer at Bretton Hall where she directs the advanced diploma in counselling. As a member of the team of researchers on the DES-funded project 'Bullying in Schools', she is involved in developing intervention strategies designed to reduce the incidence of bullying.

Stuart Dyke is presently a Staff Development Officer with Service Children's Schools (NWE). He has extensive experience of curriculum development projects, most recently with the National Writing and Oracy Projects.

Peter Geekie is Senior Lecturer in the Faculty of Education, University of Wollongong, New South Wales, Australia. For a number of years he has been a member of the Centre for Studies in Literacy at Wollongong University and was responsible for the evaluation report on the Reading Recovery Field Trail in Central Victoria in 1984.

David Gillborn is Lecturer in Education at Sheffield University. He conducted interview-based research for the Elton Committee of Enquiry into Discipline in Schools (with Jon Nixon and Jean Rudduck).

Christine Hodgkinson is a Curriculum Development Officer working on the Sheffield Low Attaining Pupils Programme (LAPP).

Eileen Baglin Jones is Assistant Education Officer with the Oxfordshire Country Council and was formerly Director of the Achievement Project. She was formerly Senior Teacher at Burford Community College and leader of the Oxfordshire New Learning Initiative Project.

Neville Jones is a Regional Tutor in Special Needs at the Open University. He was Principal Educational Psychologist with the Oxfordshire County Council Education Department from 1976 to 1990. During this period he directed the Oxfordshire Disaffected Pupil Programme and was the editor of a new series of books on Education and Alienation.

Pamela Munn is a Deputy Director of the Scottish Council for Research in Education (SCRE), where she has worked since 1986. Her research interests are in school organization and management, adult education and the professional development of teachers. She is the author of a number of publications on discipline in schools.

Peter Smith is Professor of Psychology at the University of Sheffield. He has published extensively in professional journals and is the co-author of a recent book on practical approaches to bullying.

Delwyn Tattum is Reader in Education at the Cardiff Institute of Higher Education, South Wales. He has a special interest in problems of bullying in mainstream schools and has published extensively on this topic.

Eva Tattum has taught for over 20 years in primary and secondary schools. She is particularly interested in children's social development.

Terri Webb is the Year-5 Co-ordinator at Dalton Middle School, Düsseldorf, Germany. She worked for many years as an SEN Support teacher in England and Germany.

Introduction

Books on school discipline tend to adopt one of two approaches. The first approach deals with 'incidents' in the classroom and the aim of such publications is to equip classroom teachers with some extra psychological expertise aimed at improving classroom management. The second approach addresses a much broader question of how a school develops its ethos and values. This touches on the daily school-life of all who work and learn within a school community, and focuses on a common ownership of successes as well as problems for all who work in the corporate institution we call a school. Corporate ownership carries with it corporate responsibilities and in this book the issues of discipline are seen as affecting and engaging all members of the teaching staff and others employed in the school. A corporate approach touches upon, in addition to value systems, effective school management, a meaningful curriculum for all pupils, skilled and innovative teaching and student appraisal, and takes as its starting point a preventative rather than a remedial or punishing (after the event) approach. This does not mean that schools should be without a range of sanctions, applied fairly, but such sanctions should be: well known to all concerned, who should also have been involved in coming to agreements about what the sanctions should be: governors, parents, teaching and other school employees, and pupils.

The whole-school approach advocated in this book goes some way to avoiding the arbitrary policies on discipline matters that can occur in some schools, especially where discipline is classroom-focused (as with the 'incident' approach) and takes into account interactions taking place elsewhere in the school: in corridors, the playground or in other lessons.

School discipline in general has received considerable attention in recent years arising from the Government's concern about undisciplined young people who have already left school. Schools became the scapegoats for much of the youth-led crime in inner-city areas and the growth of hooliganism and disruption at football matches. The Government was anxious to focus attention on what was believed to be considerable and widespread indiscipline in school. The Government had been encouraged in this view by certain sections of the teaching profession, who claimed

that indiscipline was rife in the schools, that there was considerable chaos and that what was required was a national enquiry.
The Government looked to its own Inspectorate to provide the
evidence in support of the claims of some teacher unions. In 1989
an HMI Working Group (DES, 1989) reported on matters related
to discipline in schools and it appeared that in the Government's
view it 'failed' to pin the disruptive aspects of student behaviour
onto methods employed in schools and teacher attitudes and
incompetence. HMI also reviewed the research that had been
carried out in recent years into discipline and pupil behaviour
(Behaviour and Discipline in School, Observed 5) and concluded
that 'violence was of very small dimension in our schools, was
often specific to particular schools, or to particular geographical
areas such as inner-city urban conglomerates'.

The Government pursued the issue of discipline by setting up
the Elton Committee (Report and Inquiry into Discipline in
Schools) which reported in 1989. The Elton Committee called for
its own research evidence and solicited, through a team at
Sheffield University, the largest survey of teachers' perceptions of
discipline in school that has been carried out in Britain. David
Gillborn was a member of the team and describes in his chapter
the ways in which classroom teachers spoke about disciplinary
issues during studies carried out in ten inner-city comprehensive
schools. Of particular interest in this chapter are the differences
in perspective about discipline issues between class teachers and
senior management in schools, and the consequent effect this has
on consistent policies within schools themselves. Gillborn reflects
on how these differences and stresses are likely to become more
'conflicting' as teachers try to cope with the 1988 legislation and
the possibility that this will lead to an increase in disciplinary
problems and a widening of the gulf between teachers and senior
management in schools.

Since the publication of the Elton Report there has been a major
study of school discipline carried out under the direction of
Pamela Munn, by the Scottish Council for Research in Education
(see details in the list of recommended reading on page 189). This
study confirms yet again the research results of other experts in
this field, namely, that there are no simple short-cuts to coping
with indiscipline, and far too often indiscipline has its roots and
cause beyond the classroom. Short-term solutions, therefore,
remedy the problem only for the limited period the pupil is in the
classroom. From the Munn research described in her chapter,
discipline matters are seen as a complex set of strategies, constraints and innovations, affecting much beyond the single 'incident' that takes place during an individual lesson.

In her chapter, Eileen Baglin Jones illustrates well how events
occurring sometimes within the school but more likely in the local
community, affect what happens in schools and teachers' percep-

tions of the 'displaced' behaviour in the context of the classroom. As Chairman of Oxfordshire's Juvenile Panel (soon to become the Youth Court), and as an experienced teacher, she has an acute awareness of the difficulties there are when teachers have to prepare informative and unbiased reports for the Court. In her account of the work she carried out to improve communication between teachers and magistrates through the simple strategy of an improved teachers' school report form, and the negotiations that took place to produce this, she reminds us that among the group of pupils who are at the centre of problems about discipline are those who are likely to be appearing before the juvenile court. For justice to be seen and practised for many of these youngsters, the liaison between magistrates and teachers is crucial, yet in most cases, the only link is in the preparation of a school report by teachers. It is upon this that magistrates have to rely in order to obtain an appreciation of what problems, or successes, there are for the defendant as far as education is concerned.

An important feature of discipline in schools is where the indiscipline takes the form of bullying. In so many cases the bullying surfaces as a conflict between one pupil and another – one the aggressor and the other the victim. What is only more recently understood is that bullying is a feature of human behaviour that can extend beyond the playground, into the staffroom, for example, so that bullying can be a teacher phenomenon too – adult with adult or adult with pupil. These elements are not as clear as the more commonplace bullying that takes place in the playground, but they do decide whether in a particular school there is a climate where bullying is likely to grow and flourish. Bullying that results in physical contact is not so insidious as bullying that is portrayed through comments and attitudes: the clever bully makes sure there is no evidence for his or her anti-social behaviour. Psychological bullying, however, can have a more dramatic consequence resulting not simply in school refusal but in pupil suicide.

Bullying is now a subject of national interest arising from the extensive studies and research that have been carried out by experts like Delwyn Tattum and the on-going research work of Helen Cowie and her colleagues at Sheffield University. The Tattums offer a detailed and informative account of the research findings on bullying behaviour and its nature as it expresses itself in the context of education. They recognize that bullying has to be approached in ways other than as a reactive cross-management response, a single reported incident, and what is required is that bullying is part of a whole-school agenda for attitudes, curriculum, and whole-school responsibility for particular vulnerable children and those who antagonize them. This chapter offers a detailed account of what could be entailed in making bullying the subject of a whole-school policy, and offers practical advice and guidance to teachers.

Helen Cowie and colleagues at Sheffield University also review the research findings, seeking as do the Tattums, an understanding of the phenomenon of bullying that can be transcribed into practical ways for schools to recognize bullying regimes, the nature of the bullying incident, and how schools can best respond. The Sheffield research tackled the problem as seen through the eyes of the pupils themselves and from this developed a range of interventions within a whole-school approach through the curriculum with the use of video, drama, story and role-play techniques. It also results in the pupils being helped to develop social skills to increase the victim's assertiveness, ability to participate in groups, co-operation and sharing.

Since the publication of the Elton Report, with its wide-ranging recommendations about school discipline, advice has poured forth from many organizations like the National Association of Head Teachers and the Health and Safety Commission. Much of this has been directed towards what headteachers and their staff can do when problem behaviour surfaces in the classroom or the school at large, or if it is thought to emanate from home or elsewhere in the community. But the focus on inappropriate behaviour in general, and bullying in particular, is on the individual pupil. What are the opportunities for pupils to learn better social skills at school and how far does the recent curriculum allow for such development? The Elton Report stressed the importance of personal and social education as a means of promoting the values of mutual respect, self-discipline and social responsibility, all of which underpin appropriate behaviour in schools. The National Curriculum Council included in its plans for cross-curriculum themes that of Education for Citizenship which would lay a foundation to help pupils acquire and understand essential information and provide them with opportunities to participate in all aspects of school life. Basic to this would be the opportunity to learn and develop skills about group behaviour, working democratically, bullying, listening to others, handling differences of opinion, and living in a pleasant society. Embedded in these ideas are opportunities to develop skills related to talking and listening, the role and function of body language, of how and when to intervene and how to use non-verbal communication. All of this helps to determine the kind of relationships we make, to express our emotions, and to handle negative social engagements. Pupils can be made aware of the power they have to control the behaviour of others and that inappropriate behaviour is often a matter of reciprocal interaction, one person to another.

A major area of educational development, as far as whole-school policies and practices are concerned, is with the application of a meaningful entitlement curriculum for all pupils. Of particular importance are those elements of the curriculum that facilitate improved pupil self-esteem, that aid pupils in the way that they think about their work, themselves and their success in school activities, that help pupils to communicate better both verbally and through body language, and provide positive reinforcement and assistance to pupils who are falling behind with their work, particularly in basic skills. There are few major studies that have not drawn attention to the connection that exists between inappropriate behaviour in school and academic performance – or lack of it.

In the final section of this book we offer the view that matters relating to discipline, in a context of whole-school policies, for the pupil in particular and the school in general, are best dealt with through appropriate curriculum approaches. This directly influences the behaviour of the pupil and is the most effective way of securing satisfactory outcomes. Christine Hodgkinson in her chapter draws attention to how the Government, in its legislation over recent years, has focused upon a curriculum, national in content, but largely irrelevant to the needs of significant proportion of pupils who require a curriculum that is meaningful to their needs and interests. She takes the opportunity to compare the objectives of a number of educational initiatives in the 1980s (the Lower Attaining Pupil Programme, LAPP, for example) with those arising from the 1988 Education Reform Act (ERA). Both aim to improve pupil performance but identical initiatives can, as far as educational objectives are concerned, create opposite outcomes. The educational initiatives of the 1980s showed that for many pupils the application of a structured curriculum is irrelevant unless there is recognition and understanding of how pupils learn in school and what makes for difficulty and failure. Central to all this is the relationship between teacher and pupil and the minutiae of daily interactions and of course work, national or otherwise. This is the context in which there are likely to be opportunities for recognition of achievement and without which no pupil sustains interest or motivation: an education that in some major parts is individualized.

The authors of this book provide a detailed account of how some of the 1980s initiatives were developed in Oxfordshire utilizing school–community links, the methods of instrumental enrichment, and residential experiences. Initially this work was part of the Government's scheme to raise achievement for pupils in their final two years of schooling (LAPP), and geared to pupils who were failing and underfunctioning. The lessons learned, however, indicated that the kind of initiatives developed in Oxfordshire, the style of management and evaluation, were equally applicable for the education of many, if not all, pupils in our schools. This led to the setting up of the Achievement Project which addressed the educational needs of all pupils in mainstream schools. Parallel with these initiatives was the Disaffected Pupil Programme aimed at identifying good practice and effective schools so that there came together a major thrust to link effective school management with innovatory teaching and a meaningful curriculum.

The 17 local education authorities who were funded by the Government to organize and run LAPP schemes used the funds in a variety of ways. A consortium of five LEAs embraced the teaching of Feurstein on thinking skills. Both Oxfordshire and Somerset LEAs worked closely together to introduce the Feurstein ideas into primary, secondary and special schools. From this initial pioneering work Oxfordshire developed its own materials for a thinking skills curriculum and Nigel Blagg was responsible for developing the Somerset Thinking Skills Course. The aims of this Course were to enhance self-esteem, promote positive attitudes and beliefs about being able to learn, and heighten awareness of learning styles as a prerequisite to learning and developing more sophisticated ways of managing one's own learning. In his chapter Nigel Blagg provides the reader not only with the rationale of the Somerset Course material, but illustrations and references for further reading. David Bowler and his colleagues in the Service Children's Educational Authority (SCEA), take the work of the Somerset Thinking Skills Course to enhance work being carried out in another curriculum area, that of the National Oracy Project. Their chapter describes a project for 9- and 10-year-old pupils aimed at improving oracy skills but coupled with this an increased social awareness and improved attitudes leading to better levels of work.

Among the variety of reading schemes available for teachers to use with slow or backward pupils, the British Government has selected the Reading Recovery (RR) programme for extensive use in primary schools. As we have indicated, the correlation between deviant behaviour and the lack of academic achievement in basic subjects has been well documented in all major surveys of pupil performance in schools. The core of pupils who fail to learn in the three Rs are nearly always part of the small population of pupils who create discipline problems for teachers. Recent surveys of reading ability in school-age children which suggest that there is more than just a small core who are failing, have prompted the Government to fund a remediation programme (RR) for a period of three years in selected schools.

The Reading Recovery programme was developed by Professor Marie Clay, of Auckland University, New Zealand. Throughout the 1980s the programme was introduced into Australia, and later the United States. It is now being introduced by LEAs in Britain and teachers, under the guidance of Professor Clay, are being trained at London University.

Peter Geekie, who was responsible for evaluating the Reading

Recovery programme in Australia, sets out in his chapter an account of precisely what the Reading Recovery programme aims to achieve, the effects the programme has on reading ability, the problems of its implementation, and some relevant comments on costing. Perhaps the key observations in Peter Geekie's contribution to this book are those where he comments that the essence of the Reading Recovery programme is not to be found in organizational structures of the scheme, but in the quality of the interaction between the teachers and the pupils. The aim of the Reading Recovery programme is not, therefore, just to produce readers, but 'self-correcting, self-regulating learners'. In essence the programme is directed to a new orientation in teaching reading rather than in the way a particular programme is organized. Peter Geekie is clear in his mind that 'every system should strive to teach all children to read and write . . .' but there should be a turning away 'from debates about methodology of basic literacy instruction, to how we might best meet the challenge of giving (pupils) full access to the culture of literacy'.

The views put forward by Peter Geekie about the aims of learning, in whatever context and towards whatever objectives, is consistent with approaches taken by many contributors to this book. Whatever managerial structures are required to deliver a system of education, its value falls by the wayside when that system does not embrace the interactional skills, energies, and interests of all who do the teaching and all who are the learners. Whole-school approaches, whether about discipline matters or any other activity in a school, encompass this central theme that quality education and effective schooling begins with a corporate approach to all the daily vicissitudes in the life of school, which then translates itself into individual interactions, pupil and pupil, pupil and teacher. We are tempted to agree with W. Edwards Deming, the American management guru, who declares 'Quality is about people not products' and encourages the kind of focus on a consideration of values and relationships between people engaged together in an enterprise, which is tacitly subscribed to by many of the contributors in this volume. When there is a true acknowledgement that in schools the day-to-day stuff of people working alongside each other is what matters most, this is where the issue of discipline, among so many other issues in the life of a school, takes its place and not in some narrow method of organization and control of individual pupil behaviour.

(*See* p. 189 for References)

Part One: Support and Management of Pupil Behaviour

Chapter 1

Ways of Improving Discipline in Secondary Schools and Classrooms

Pamela Munn

INTRODUCTION

Discipline in schools has long been a concern to teachers, parents, politicians and education authorities. Over a hundred years ago, when government grants to schools were based on a payments by results system, part of the payment was earmarked for classroom organisation and discipline. Teachers got 1/6d per child if classroom organization and discipline were excellent; 1/- if they were good; and the possibility of nothing at all if they were less than good. At the present time teachers are no longer offered extrinsic rewards for good discipline but concern about it is still very much in evidence. There have been two major committees of enquiry: the Pack Committee (1977) reported on truancy and discipline in Scottish schools and the more recent Elton Committee (1989) investigated the nature and extent of discipline problems facing teachers in England and Wales. Furthermore, there are many books offering advice to teachers about classroom discipline, suggesting that new teachers shouldn't 'smile until Christmas', and identifying a range of approaches which experienced teachers have found effective. The continuing popularity of these text suggest beginning teachers, at any rate, are in search of recipes which will ensure effective discipline in their classrooms. As every experienced teacher knows, such recipes do not exist. Instead, each school and teacher adopt a range of strategies which seem appropriate to their own particular circumstances and which are more or less effective. Schools operate in particular contexts with their own histories and what works in one school or classroom will not necessarily work in another. Indeed, what works with one teacher may not work with another, teaching the same class.

There is broad agreement among writers on discipline that what counts as effective discipline is heavily dependent on the context in which a teacher is operating. The age and stage of the pupils, the time of day, the time of year, the content of the lesson and many other factors can all influence what counts as effective discipline. For example, what counts as effective discipline for a teacher working with a group of first year pupils would be rather different from the discipline standard expected of sixth years. Similarly, what counts as effective discipline first thing on a Monday morning, might be different from last thing on a Friday afternoon. So, the same teacher can have different standards of discipline; teachers in the same school can have different standards; the teachers in different schools can have different standards. Schools differ too, in the kinds of rules they highlight and in the ways they encourage good discipline. Recent research on school effectiveness has suggested that schools are social institutions whose nature and climate have important influences on the behaviour, attitudes and attainments of pupils.

Where does this leave us in our search for effective discipline? First of all it highlights the futility of the quest for a universal answer to discipline problems. Secondly, however, an understanding of how schools operate their discipline policy and why they do so in particular ways can sensitize us to important influences on their practice. Being alert to these influences is the key starting point for schools wanting to improve their discipline. Only by understanding why their current practice is the way it is, can schools begin to plan real and lasting improvements.

This chapter is intended to help schools review their own policy and practice by describing what a small number of secondary schools in a research study did. In describing these schools' practice – practice seen as effective by the teachers and pupils in them – it is not the intention that others should mimic their behaviour. We know that what works in one school will not necessarily work in another. Rather, by pin-pointing reasons for their practice, the chapter offers starting points for schools to examine what they necessarily have to take for granted in the hurly-burly of school life.

THE RESEARCH

The research took place in four comprehensive schools in different parts of Scotland. It involved interviewing teachers about school discipline policy and practice, asking pupils to write about discipline, analysing school documents and collecting field notes. The study of whole school discipline was complemented by a study of classroom discipline. This involved the intensive study of 16 teachers, getting them to describe what they did to get the class to work well. While the focus of the classroom work was wide, the whole school aspects were structured by asking about the following:

- school rules, sanctions and rewards
- whether common standards were applied by staff
- the role of pastoral care.

The intensive work in four schools enabled us to explore what their discipline policy and practice were and to understand the influences on that practice. We report these influences as starting points for debate and discussion in schools interested in reviewing their discipline. They are not necessarily transferable and the schools are not representative of all schools in the United Kingdom. So what were the key influences on school policy and practice?

KEY INFLUENCES ON WHOLE SCHOOL DISCIPLINE POLICY

The research revealed five key influences on school discipline:

- the school's view of its pupils;
- what teachers saw as the main purposes of teaching;
- the role of senior management; and
- the extent to which subject departments were free to set their own discipline standards.

These influences emerged from interviews with teachers, analysis of school documents and observation of classrooms and of school life. These are areas which schools need to address if they want to improve discipline. Their influence on the research schools is described only to illustrate and to provoke discussion and debate. The small number of schools involved in the research means that they cannot be seen as representative or typical. Their practice may strike chords with your own experience or alternatively seem strange. Whatever the effect, the intention is to encourage a fresh look at your school, approaching it as a stranger, taking little for granted and using the experience of the schools reported here as a beginning of an investigation into what your school's discipline policy and practice are and why they are that way.

The school's view of its pupils

The idea that schools view their pupils in distinctively different ways may seem rather contentious. After all, schools in Britain have the same broad general aims for pupils. In the case of secondary schools these can be summed up as promoting academic achievement, preparing pupils for working life, educating the young for rational autonomy and social interdependence (Hargreaves, 1989). How can it be then, that schools view their pupils in particular and distinctive ways? The answer to this question lies in the subtle degrees of emphasis given to certain aims rather than to others. One school, for instance, saw its pupils predominantly as scholars, there to make progress through the academic curriculum and achieve success in public examinations. The pupils were there to learn and the teachers were there to teach and that was all there was to it. Let a teacher from Oldtown Grammar convey this view:

> I feel the children know what to expect . . . we know from the past, they're motivated and ready to learn, they've been conditioned to learn.

Some other schools saw their pupils as lacking in social skills, believed they could do something about these skills, and saw their pupils predominantly as members of the school family. The social and emotional growth of pupils was stressed as much as their scholastic achievement. This view was neatly summed up by a teacher from St James, a Roman Catholic school, situated in an area of multiple deprivation:

> The children on the whole are nice kids. They find school a bit of a haven where the rigours of home life can be left behind. They treat staff almost as members of an extended family.

The school view could be gleaned not only from teachers talking about their pupils but from their brochures and discipline policy documents. Oldtown's brochure, for instance, stressed the prizes and trophies for scholastic and sporting achievement; listed the full academic qualifications of its staff and gave considerable space to such matters as the formal curriculum, methods of assessment, and the importance of homework to 'foster the habit of study'. Whereas another school's brochure stressed the extended family nature of the enterprise, as follows:

> The young people of the area are the responsibility of school, parents and community. School interest does not cease at 4.00 pm; the community interest should not cease at 9.00 am . . . It is only by working together, by appreciating each other's work and problems that we can meet the aims of the school and make ours a happy, efficient community.

So how did a school's view of its pupils influence discipline? Obvious features of school discipline are school rules, sanctions and rewards. In Oldtown, where the emphasis was on the pupil as scholar, there were a few rules; about dress – pupils were expected to be neat and tidy in appearance – courtesy and general behaviour. The school took it for granted that pupils knew how to behave and did not need rules to be spelt out to them. They copied out the rules in their books and were not encouraged to debate or discuss them. As one teacher remarked:

> Yes, the [pupils] do [respect the rules]. They're never encouraged not to. There's not an atmosphere of questioning the rules.

In contrast, St James' staff believed they could not take acceptable behaviour for granted. The school rules were conveyed through the school's social education programme. These were more specific than Oldtown's and, crucially, time was taken to explain the rationale for rules in general and for specific rules. The staff believed that pupils would readily stick to the rules once they understood why they were necessary.

Schools have broadly similar sanctions available to them which can be brought into play when rules are broken. These range from verbal rebukes and perhaps isolation within the classroom for minor offences to punishment exercises or detention for more serious offences and ultimately to suspension or exclusion from school. All our research schools operated a line management system whereby offending pupils could be referred to successively more senior staff and ultimately to the headteacher. How, then, did the school's view of its pupils affect the sanctions used?

In Oldtown pupil misbehaviour was not expected. When it did happen the main concern was that it should not distort the work ethos of the school. Exclusion from class involved pupils doing specified work in the administration block out of sight of other pupils and staff. Punishment was private and solitary and very much work oriented. In St James, a miscreant usually found him/herself engaged in some socially useful activity, such as picking up litter round the school. The supervisory teacher saw this as an opportunity to get to know the pupil and, hopefully, come to understand the reason for bad behaviour. Furthermore, the behaviour card was used differently, according to their view of the pupils. This card is carried by pupils who have misbehaved and each teacher signs the card and gives a mark and/or comment about behaviour. In St James it was used sparingly, involved contacting parents and was seen as a way of supporting pupils who were trying to reform. In Oldtown, each subject department could issue a card and it was seen as a way of establishing good work habits.

Oldtown's emphasis on its pupils as scholars meant that behaviour which challenged the work ethic was punished by reinforcing the importance of the ethic. In St James, bad behaviour was punished not so much be reinforcing the work ethic but by reinforcing the notion of the school as a community where reasons for bad behaviour were explored and support offered to do better.

It is well documented that teachers are not much given to praising and rewarding pupils. There were few rewards in evidence specifically for good behaviour and those that were, reflected the school's view of its pupils. St James had a merit league for its younger pupils. Each class was awarded points for good work and good behaviour and the class with the highest score was given a treat, such as a school trip, or a party. The reward focused on the behaviour of the class and so was congruent with the community emphasis in the school. This contrasted with prize-giving at Oldtown where the reward was for individual endeavour in academics or sport.

These brief examples of the impact of a school's view of its pupils are designed to provoke discussion. Staff and pupils in each school saw discipline as working effectively. Of course, as in all human affairs, there were benefits and costs to the particular approaches used and it is not the intention to portray one school's policy as preferable to another. Rather, the intention is to raise awareness of how any school views its pupils and the impact of such views on its rules, sanctions and rewards systems. There are many more views of pupils than the two described here.

What view of pupils does your school hold? The following activities can help you find out:

- Read the school brochure as if you were a stranger. What kinds of expectations of pupils does it convey? Are these as you intend? If not, what changes are needed?
- Look at the school rules. Are the published rules seen as really the important ones? What kind of expectations do they convey – good behaviour or bad behaviour?
- What messages are conveyed to staff, pupils and parents by the way sanctions are used by senior staff?
- Does the school have any rewards for good behaviour or is the emphasis on bad behaviour being punished?
- Find out what pupils think. Ask a group to write about school rules, rewards and punishments.
- What do you see as the benefits and costs of Oldtown and St James' views of their pupils? How do these compare with your own school's situation?

Teachers' views of the purposes of teaching

Just as schools share the same broad aims for their pupils, so teachers tend to share the same broad view of the purposes of teaching. These can be summed up as pupils learning what it is intended they should learn, and developing each pupil to his or her potential. However, teaching does not take place in a vacuum. Many different kinds of influence are brought to bear on what is taught and how it is taught and a key influence, unsurprisingly, is what teachers know about their pupils. This affects the kinds of goals which teachers see as realistic and achievable for their pupils, which in turn affects what counts as good discipline in classrooms. For example, a teacher who knows that her upper sixth class of A-level students is well motivated and able would have distinctive goals for the class concerned not only with the standard of its work but with the way the class would behave during lessons. Of course, the knowledge which teachers have about their pupils is not necessarily accurate or complete but, as we shall see when we look at classroom discipline below, it is a profound influence on teachers' actions. For the moment, we wish to suggest that the school's view of its pupils affects the broad goals which teachers see as realistic for the pupils and so sets the general framework for classroom discipline.

At Oldtown Grammar, where pupils were viewed predominantly as scholars, teachers talked about work-related goals for their pupils and the framework for classroom discipline was that pupils should be getting on with their academic work. One Oldtown teacher explained that 'Pupils are here to learn . . . that's the long and short of it really. . . . Behaviour which is irrelevant to the working pattern just should not happen'. At another school, Braidburn, where the pupil was viewed as a member of the school family, teachers talked about the need to motivate pupils to learn. The local community was not one where the academic curriculum was valued. Pupils had to be persuaded of its value when they came to school and this was translated into general teaching goals about motivation, interest and enjoyment in learning. Teachers talked about 'zinging it to the pupils', 'making the lesson come alive'. The framework for classroom discipline was one which recognized the need to motivate children to learn, a state of affairs which Oldtown could largely take for granted. Hence, affective goals, concerning children's interest and enthusiasm, were at least as important as progressing through a set curriculum. A comment from a teacher gives a flavour of what counted as effective discipline:

> They're working because they're all engaged. . . . Rather than getting a pupil to sit down and copy – and pupils are quite happy to do that – I don't allow that, it's not educational. . . . They must develop the skill to describe the practical work in their own words and [eventually] they do it quite well.

It is possible to infer from the above extract, that one influence on the goals which the teacher sets is previous experience. He knows that eventually pupils will be able to write up practicals in their own words. Another influence is clearly his belief about the efficacy of certain teaching methods – 'I don't allow [copying from the blackboard or from books] its not educational'. The influence of the school view of its pupils is more difficult to trace directly as is the way in which it conveys itself to staff. However, an analysis of the broad goals which teachers in the various case-study schools had for their pupils, suggested that Oldtown teachers, for example, talked largely in terms of pupils working hard and quietly accepting the material of the lesson, whereas teachers at St James and Braidburn tended to stress active engagement with materials, developing confidence in their pupils and encouraging pupils to be on their toes.

What is the dominant view of the purposes of teaching in your school? The following activities can help you find out.

- Think about the rules you see as being most important with a particular class. Keep a diary, on tape or in notes, of the rules you have communicated to the class over a week, through reminders and the use of sanctions when rules are broken, for instance. In what other ways might your views of the most important classroom rules be conveyed to pupils?
- How do these rules compare and contrast with school rules? What explanations for match and mismatch can you offer?
- Ask the pupils to write about your classroom rules and to identify those which affect them most.
- Discuss your diary and your analysis of pupils' writing with colleagues. Do they have similar views?
- How do your findings relate to the school view of its pupils?

The influence of departmental and teacher autonomy on discipline

One of the striking differences among the research schools was the degree to which subject departments were free to 'run their own ship' as far as standards of discipline were concerned. In two schools, departments had considerable freedom to extend and develop the general school rules to suit their own circumstances. These schools operated a system of extended autonomy. Teachers in these schools felt that colleagues outside their own departments had different definitions of good discipline and different ways of dealing with indiscipline. In contrast, our other pair of schools operated a system of restricted departmental autonomy. Staff in these schools talked about common approaches to discipline. Although there were a few references to special rules, such as safety rules in the science department, there was a general assumption that all departments had the same rules.

How was discipline affected? In Oldtown, extended departmental autonomy seemed a natural way of working in a school where scholastic achievement was highly valued. The departments were the locus of subject expertise and so it was entirely logical and consistent that they should also define what counted as good discipline when pupils were in the department. The main benefit was the explicit recognition of the importance and professionalism of the subject department and the status of the head of department as a 'middle manager' with considerable independence while the main cost was that it could lead to different standards in different departments. Another cost could be the dominance of departmental concerns to the detriment of discipline in corridors and playgrounds. In Braidburn, restricted autonomy reinforced the notion of the school as a close-knit community. The benefits were that pupils were aware of common expectations about behaviour across the curriculum, teachers felt secure in enforcing rules because they were the school rules, and rules were enforced both outside and inside the classroom. The costs were in terms of the professional autonomy of staff if they felt that rules, sanctions and rewards had not been thoroughly discussed and agreed. Such consultation can be seen as a cost in senior management time, especially if disagreements are revealed and persuasion and cajoling of staff to accept a common standard are needed.

The autonomy of the individual teachers to define their own standards of discipline could be constrained under either system of extended or restricted departmental autonomy. A department with the freedom to run its own ship may grant extended autonomy in turn to the individual teachers in the department to set their own standards of discipline. Other departments, however, saw each individual teacher in the department as part of a close-knit team, following a standard pattern. One teacher commented with approval that '[These are] rules that have been made as a department and I carry them through almost to the letter of the law, obviously, you have to'.

Where teachers were operating either in a departmental or a school-wide system of restricted autonomy they could feel that they were to blame if they had a persistent problem with a pupil or class. The pressure of general expectations in the school, the similarities among departments in dealing with indiscipline and staff discussion of what counted as good discipline could all combine to put pressure on a teacher having discipline problems. One teacher gives the flavour of this kind of cost: 'It's not the child that's at fault but your teaching. So it's not the child who is dealt with. [This means that] you're perceived as weak by the class. It makes life a lot tougher'. As with earlier sections on the school's view of its pupils and the main purposes of teaching emphasized by the staff, it is not the intention to suggest that restricted autonomy is more effective than extended autonomy or vice versa. Each system had benefits and costs and each was seen as effective in the schools mentioned.

How would you characterize autonomy in your school? Would you agree that different departments have different standards of discipline – or do you feel that departments tend to operate in the same way? Find out more about the autonomy operating in your school by, for example:

- Comparing rules and regulations across a range of subject departments. Are there important differences among them?
- Think of an example where a colleague dealt with a discipline problem in an unexpected way. What happended? Was this recognized as an acceptable demonstration of professional independence? Challenged by the headteacher? Glossed over? What does it tell you about the kind of autonomy operating in the school?
- What do you see as the benefits and costs of your current system in respect of discipline?
- Why do you think the system is as it is? Does it harmonize with other aspects of discipline policy?

Management systems

The final influence on whole school discipline which emerged from researching the schools was that of management. Teachers would say that of course good management helps, bad management hinders. However, a school's management team operates in a real context and what is good in one context may not be good in another. We do not intend to develop a picture of an ideal management system. Rather, we want to suggest that the way senior staff go about the task of managing gives messages about what counts as good discipline. A school interested in reviewing its discipline policy and practice needs to investigate the role that senior staff play in promoting good discipline and in dealing with indiscipline.

Among our research schools, two distinctive management systems emerged. One pair of schools operated what we have called a strict line management system. In other words, basic standards of discipline were set out in a discipline policy statement which also delineated 'standard' responses to indiscipline, heads of department were responsible for promoting and maintaining discipline within their own department and only serious offences were dealt with by senior management. The other pair of schools adopted a more informal, open approach, encouraging discussion of discipline among staff. Although badly behaved pupils could be referred up the hierarchy from class teacher to senior staff, these senior staff were highly visible around the school and could intervene in the handling of minor offences. The system was characterized by flexibility, the referral chain for bad behaviour being extended or shortened as circumstances required. For such a flexible system to work, a high degree of consensus on the kinds of offences requiring an urgent or more relaxed response had to exist. If it hadn't, senior staff ran the risk of being overloaded with minor problems.

The headteacher occupies a special position among senior staff. As far as discipline is concerned, he or she can set the tone and, of course, there is a special role for the headteacher in excluding pupils from school. Staff in the research schools highlighted the personality and visibility of the head as important in promoting good discipline rather than talking about aspects of leadership. Where headteachers were visible around the school, accessible to teachers and pupils and generally approachable, this was valued by both. When pupils wrote about their headteacher it was in terms of enforcing the rules, rather than promoting positive feelings. The head was the ultimate sanction and pupils wrote with approval of their heads personally making sure rules were kept. Where headteachers were less visible, more office-based, this was seen, particularly by staff, as lack of interest in how class teachers were dealing with discipline. Being visible, friendly and accessible is no guarantee of effective discipline. It is noteworthy, however, that the presence of these attributes was favourably mentioned in unprompted interviews, and their absence regretted.

The kinds of strategies used by headteachers and senior staff to promote good discipline included:

- regular assemblies of all the pupils;
- setting up a merit league to reward good discipline among younger pupils;
- contacting parents with good news and praise of pupils;
- learning the names of all the pupils, to let them know they belonged;
- being visible around the school, being seen to be interested in the pupils and in good discipline;
- experimenting with the curriculum to meet the needs of as many different pupils as possible; and
- offering a wide range of extra-curricular activities.

The schools differed in the nature and extent of the measures used. Where they were similar was in the belief that they could affect their pupils' behaviour; that schools did make a difference.

What are the implications for schools wanting to review their discipline policy and practice? Either management approach can be effective. Those interested in discipline management could consider some of the following activities.

- Keep a note of the head and/or senior staff's visibility around the school during one week. Where did they appear? In what circumstances? Who did they talk to? Were there spin-offs for discipline?

- Analyse an instance where senior staff and teachers communicated successfully about a discipline incident, and ask:
  What made it successful?
  Who was involved?
  Was anyone left out? Why?
- Take a typical referral of a problem up the hierarchy. Why was it referred? Who referred it? Did things work out well for teachers and pupils? Why?
- Does your school tend towards line management or informal management? Analyse the benefits and costs of your school's management system.

CLASSROOM DISCIPLINE

To understand how teachers went about promoting effective discipline in their classrooms we studied 16 secondary teachers, four teachers in each of the research schools. These teachers differed from each other in many ways – they taught different subjects, had gone to different training colleges, had been teaching for different lengths of time and some were male, some female. What they had in common, however, was an approach to promoting classroom discipline. This approach, elicited from their own accounts of their practice, mirrored the advice given in many texts. It consisted of:

- advance planning and preparation to avoid disruption;
- reaction to disruption or to threats of it by using a variety of techniques;
- using their knowledge of individual pupils and the class as a whole to select an appropriate method of discipline; and
- being sensitive to a range of influences on their effectiveness, such as time of day or the subject matter of the lesson.

The teachers studied were chosen on the basis of pupils' views of the teachers who were best at getting the class to work well. The pupils identified a wide variety of actions as effective and did not present an ideal or stereotype of an effective disciplinarian. Teachers similarly talked about a number of different actions they took, actions which were heavily dependent on the school and classroom context in which they were working. In reporting teachers' descriptions of what they did, we are not suggesting others mimic their specific practice. Rather, we are suggesting that teachers, teacher educators and others use the framework presented as a way of highlighting awareness about what teachers do and why they do it. It is important to make clear that we are reporting teachers' talk about their actions, not observation of their practice. This was because we wanted to get at teachers' own ideas of what was effective, rather than their reactions to our ideas of what had worked. The teachers were observed teaching two different classes over a fortnight. At the end of each observed lesson we asked, 'What did you do to get the class to work well?' Teachers found this a very difficult question to answer as we were asking them to make explicit their routine, taken-for-granted and spontaneous behaviour.

Preventing disruption

When our 16 teachers talked about the kinds of things which they had done to get particular classes to work well, it soon became apparent that they did some things in advance of the pupils ever appearing in their classrooms. For example, they would make sure they were in the classroom before the pupils arrived, or materials were laid out ready, or that they had viewed a video in advance of using it as a teaching aid and had planned how to use it. All these kinds of actions we called 'proactive'. They were taken to avoid opportunities for disruption occurring. They included advance preparation and planning and setting out clearly the framework in which pupils would operate. This included establishing routines for entering and leaving the classroom, homework completion and specific rules about, for example, talking or moving about the classroom. It also included giving clear instructions and organizing work so that pupils knew what they were expected to do. Being proactive then, means that teachers prepare things in advance, they do not wait for something to happen to prevent the class from working well before taking action. Over 50 per cent of teachers' talk about what they did to get their class to work well was about proactive approaches.

In contrast to being proactive, some actions were triggered by a sign or signs. Here the teacher is responding to a cue that a pupil, a group, or the class as a whole are not working well. These responding type of actions we called 'reactive'. For example, a teacher describes his reaction to a cue that one girl was not working well:

> I was very aware of one girl talking. She was playing with a mirror. I watched her for about 5 seconds. . . . She realized . . . and got on with her work.

It was noteworthy that over 30 per cent of the actions taken by these experienced teachers and effective disciplinarians concerned reacting to threats of disruption. This suggests that discipline is not something that can be established once and for all in a classroom. It requires constant monitoring and reinforcement. The kinds of actions taken varied enormously. They included using humour, issuing threats, moving pupils to the front of the classroom and standing alongside a pupil to encourage concentration. No action or group of actions dominated. Once again the context in which the teacher was working strongly influenced their reaction to disruption.

How do teachers know what actions to take?

There are two main influences on teachers' actions, the conditions or context in which they are operating and the goals they have for their pupils and class. Let us look at each in turn.

The context in which teaching is carried out has a profound effect on what teachers do and on what they count as getting the class to work well. Teachers talked to us about a number of aspects of context which affected their actions. These included the time of day, or year, the nature of the subject, beliefs about teaching and the numbers of pupils in the class. By far the largest percentage of their talk about contextual aspects – over 40 per cent – concerned their knowledge of the class as a whole or their knowledge of an individual pupil. Knowledge of a pupil might include knowledge of the home background, the pupil's behaviour in school in previous years or the pupil's abilities. Teacher knowledge was not necessarily accurate or complete but it seemed to be a profound influence on the kind of actions they took to get the class to work well. In the following example the teacher explains his action, having a 'wee chat' very quietly with a pupil, in terms of his knowledge of that pupil:

> He [pupil] is very backward. . . . He tends to be the butt of many of the other pupils' jokes. . . . I feel sorry for the boy. I think he responds to a quiet word, rather than a shout or a loud command. . . . I had a wee chat quietly in his ear . . . that unless [his behaviour] improved he'd be sitting beside me.

There are many conditions which influence teachers' actions and these reinforce the notion that general principles of how to proceed in maintaining classroom discipline are more easily identified than specific actions which are guaranteed to work.

A further influence on the actions teachers take is the goal or goals which they have for their classes. There are things which the teacher hopes will be achieved during the course of the lesson or as the end result of the lesson. Goals can include getting through a piece of work, producing an artefact, carrying out an experiment successfully and so on. Furthermore, teachers are likely to have goals for particular pupils. A frequently mentioned goal in this category is to encourage pupils to answer a question without feeling foolish if the answer is wrong. One teacher, for example, stressed 'I take daft answers as well as good answers because I don't like to discourage anyone from answering out'. Goals can be in conflict and can assume different orders of priority. We came across some examples of teachers who reacted differently to pupils' breaking the same classroom rules, because of goal conflict. One teacher's decision to punish one pupil and let another off being punished for forgetting to bring their books was affected by his knowledge of the pupils and his goal of wanting to encourage one of the pupils, an habitual truant, to keep coming to school. This goal conflicted with his desire to be seen to be fair with all pupils:

> He's [pupil x] low ability, an awful nice wee lad. We're lucky if we get him to school each day, so I'm bending the rules with him which is a bit unfair. [Pupil y] is a rascal of the first order. . . . He's just at it.

Goals, conditions and actions all interact and it is this which makes it difficult to satisfy beginning teachers' demands for recipe knowledge about maintaining classroom discipline. It seems likely that experienced teachers are expert at matching goals and conditions. They also have a repertoire of actions which they can use to plan to avoid disruption and to react to cues that the class is not working well. These actions, it seems, are built up through experience. No particular action or set of actions emerged as dominant among the 16 teachers in terms of a reaction to the class not working well. What did emerge was the emphasis on advance preparation and planning to avoid disruption.

How can the framework be used?

The simple framework of goals, conditions and actions can be used as an aid to teachers reflecting on their own practice, or perhaps, more importantly, as a guide for student teachers observing experienced teachers in action. For example, distinctions could be attempted between the proactive and reactive and influences on actions could be detected by noting a teacher's references to contextual features. There are obvious limits to what can be gleaned from observation alone. One of the heartening aspects of our research was teachers' increasing ability to talk about their practice in response to an open question and on the basis of a shared experience of a lesson. Teachers may have become adept during the research at providing rationalizations rather than 'true explanations' but the consistency and face validity of their accounts make this doubtful. In an era when increasing attention is being given to the 'practical' and 'relevant' aspects of teacher education programmes, it is important that experienced teachers' craft knowledge is elicited and described. Teachers can describe what they do in real lessons in response to non-judgmental and positive questioning. Is this an approach which could be exploited in teaching practice?

CONCLUSION

The theme of this chapter is that there is no magic way of improving discipline in secondary schools and classrooms. What counts as good discipline in one context will not be appropriate for another context. However, we believe that our research has indicated some key areas which schools could begin to address if they want to improve discipline. These are:

- the school's expectations of its pupils;
- what teachers see as the main purpose of teaching;
- the degree of autonomy given to subject departments and individual teachers to set their own discipline standards; and
- management approaches.

Similarly, in classroom discipline the key points are:

- advance preparation and planning;
- having a repertoire of actions to bring into play when disruption is threatened or takes place; and
- being expert at matching goals, conditions and actions.

Transforming school or classroom discipline is no easy task and is a task which goes to the heart of the way the school and teachers see themselves. This is not to suggest that teachers wring their hands and say nothing can be done to improve discipline. It is to suggest that is requires considerable commitment and motivation and that ways ahead have to be rooted in a school understanding why its current practice is the way it is. Once a school begins to investigate its own practice and to pinpoint its strengths and weaknesses, then it can engage in discussion and debate on the likely benefits and costs of any changes, using the examples here as a starting point.

NOTE: The research reported here was funded by the Scottish Office Education Department (SOED) and undertaken in collaboration with Margaret Johnstone and Valerie Chalmers. The views contained in the article are those of the author and not necessarily those of SOED or the Scottish Council for Research in Education.

REFERENCES

Department of Education and Science (1989) *Discipline in School* (The Elton Report), London: HMSO.
Hargreaves, D H (1989) 'Introduction' in Jones, N (ed.) *School Management and Pupil Behaviour* Lewes: Falmer Press.
Scottish Education Department (1977) *Truancy and Indiscipline in Schools in Scotland* (Pack Report), Edinburgh: SED.

Chapter 2

Management and Teachers – Discipline and Support

David Gillborn

INTRODUCTION

In this chapter I examine the ways in which classroom teachers and their senior management spoke about disciplinary issues during interview-based research in ten inner-city comprehensive schools. The notion of 'support' emerged as a key concept for both groups, yet the precise meanings and uses of the term differed such that senior management felt they could not always offer *absolute* (total) support. Crucially, there was a conflict between senior staff's desire to react flexibly as they saw fit, and the classroom teachers' concern that their colleagues' responses to indiscipine should be both visible and predictable. This conflict reflected the structural location and interests of the two groups and has important implications for staff morale and management–teacher relationships.

THE BACKGROUND TO THE RESEARCH

This chapter is based on 100 taped interviews with a range of teachers and their headteachers in ten inner-city comprehensive schools in the English North and Midlands. The interviews took place during the Autumn term of 1988 and formed part of a co-ordinated research project funded by the Department of Education and Science (DES) as part of the work of the Committee of Enquiry into Discipline in Schools, chaired by Lord Elton (DES/WO, 1989). Two related projects were undertaken. First, a nationally representative postal survey of teachers' views on discipline – the largest of its kind ever conducted in this country (Gray and Sime, 1989). Secondly, a team of researchers visited ten inner-city comprehensives, which had not taken part in the postal survey, to interview teachers on a one-to-one basis concerning their experiences and perceptions of discipline (Gillborn *et al.*, 1989).[1] The classroom teachers were chosen to represent the full range of staff characteristics and experiences including both sexes, different levels of responsibility, greater and lesser teaching experience, varying time served in the school and different subject specialisms.[2]

The interviews were semi-structured: this reflected a deliberate attempt to maximize comparability between the different schools whilst retaining the flexibility necessary to allow teachers to discuss the aspects of disclipine which *they* felt were most important.

TALKING ABOUT DISCIPLINE: 'MANAGEMENT' AND 'TEACHER' DISCOURSE

Our visits to schools generated a great deal of data. Analysis of the interview transcipts highlighted the complex nature of disciplinary issues and revealed certain key themes which were common across the ten schools. Teachers in each of the schools, for example, mentioned the importance of curriculum content, flexible pedagogical approaches and good links with pupils' families and communities. In addition, teachers shared a concern with the cumulative effects of frequent and wearing acts of indiscipline which (although apparently trivial when viewed in isolation) could eventually place staff under enormous physical and emotional strain (Gillborn, *et al.*, 1989).

Although these important themes emerged in each of the schools we visited, there were, of course, numerous differences in the experiences and perceptions of staff in different schools, subject departments and positions of responsibility. Many of these differences reflected particular circumstances and incidents in the histories of the individual schools and interviewees; it was also possible, however, to discern more regular patterns in the views and concerns of certain interviewees. These differences may be particularly important where they reflect the contrasting, sometimes conflicting, interests, goals and values of participants who occupy different locations within the institutional structure of the school.

In this chapter I want to focus on the ways in which teachers spoke about discipline and the terms in which they described the action that should be taken when discipline is breached. I will outline two related but fundamentally contrasting disciplinary *discourses*: where 'discourse' is understood as 'a particular area of language use [which] may be identified by the institutions to which it relates and by the position from which it comes and which it marks out for the speaker' (Macdonell, 1986, pp. 2–3).

I will concentrate on the differences which emerged between the discourses of (a) those staff who spent most of their timetable engaged in classroom teaching, and (b) those members of the senior management team (SMT) who spent much less time in the classroom and were often taken up with larger scale administrative, curricular and pastoral activities. I will argue that despite many similarities, the teacher and management discourses were fundamentally opposed because of a dilemma between the need for 'consistency' and the need for 'flexibility'.

TEACHER DISCOURSE

In this section I focus on a group of staff whose discourse concerning disciplinary issues shared certain key themes and seemed to stem from their lived experience and sense of identity as classroom teachers. A basic criterion which separated these people from others in the school was that they spent the majority of their daily timetable in classroom teaching situations. This is, of course, a very heterogeneous grouping which accounted for the majority of all staff in the ten schools which we visited. The group included people who ranged from the basic main professional grade (MPG) through to those receiving incentive allowances for special responsibilities, including heads of subject departments. Of course, not all staff who fell within this group spoke about discipline in the same way: there were some classroom teachers who did not share this perspective. In general, however, the views and concerns which I refer to as 'teacher discourse' were widely shared.[3]

The importance of disciplinary issues

A recently revised document by Her Majesty's Inspectors (HMI) begins with the statement that 'Good behaviour is a necessary condition for effective teaching and learning to take place . . . ' (HMI, 1989, para. 1). Few of our interviewees would disagree. For many of the classroom teachers we spoke with, both during interviews and informally around the school, discipline was a major concern: as one teacher put it, 'If I didn't have good discipline I'd have packed it in long ago' (F 11/11 MPG+incentive allowance English).

The problem of establishing and maintaining good behaviour and discipline seems especially pressing for those starting out on a career in teaching (Lacey, 1977; Connell, 1985). For younger and less experienced teachers disciplinary issues can come to dominate their view of school life:

> Discipline's a really big worry when you first start in your first teaching job, a bigger worry than anything else, because if you can't get control of the class you can't teach anything. I remember for me that was the sort of *one thing*, you know, which really worried me . . . . (F 2/2 MPG special needs)

Now embarking on her third year in teaching, this interviewee had already gained considerable confidence in her classroom management skills. However, she remained uneasy about the amount of discretion involved in identifying and acting against breaches of schools rules:

> If there was a set of things like, 'This is what you do to a child who's done this' or 'This is what you do when . . .' *To make it clear cut*, so you'd know that certain things you deal with it this way, certain other things should be dealt with in another way. (F 2/2 MPG special needs)

Many classroom teachers, sometimes of very great experience, echoed this plea for more guidance and 'consistency' in the identification and punishment of indiscipline. In fact, this theme was a familiar part of teacher discourse. With their growing experience and confidence, discipline ceased to be an obsessive concern for most classroom teachers, yet they still held strong views as to the proper way to achieve and maintain discipline. In particular, classroom teachers seemed to have a fairly stable and clearly articulated set of expectations concerning the actions which senior management, especially headteachers, should take in order to support them.

Teachers' concerns: key concepts in teacher discourse

Support
One of teachers' most basic expectations is that senior management, *especially headteachers*, should give them support (Earley, 1989). In the ten comprehensive schools which we visited, support was understood in many different ways. One of the most fundamental aspects of SMT support concerned their response when teachers complained of disciplinary problems, especially where parents were involved. In such cases, the head was expected to accept the teachers' version of events:

> [When a pupil accused the teacher of physical violence] I wasn't really given any support. The head at that time was listening to the lad, he wasn't sort of listening to *my side of it*. And I felt I wasn't really given the right kind of support on that occasion. I don't think I was in any way guilty – unless you can say putting your hand on kid's shoulder is a criminal act. (M 22/5 MPG+incentive allowance design)

> If you are experiencing difficulties then you actually do need support from senior colleagues. I mean the 'He's alright with me' syndrome is not much help if he ain't alright with you. And it isn't an argument either, you can't have that sort of thing, you need people who are actually going to come in and support you by either taking action – if that's what it requires – or

whatever . . . . (F 20/13 MPG+incentive allowance cross curricular)

The requirement that management colleagues should 'back the teacher up' seems to be an almost universal part of teacher culture. Becker (1951; 1953), for example, found that school teachers in post-war Chicago required absolute public support from their principals, regardless of the legitimacy of the teachers' action. Becker quotes the following:

> [during a case conference] the principal had the nerve to say to the parent that she couldn't understand the difficulty, none of the other teachers who had the child had ever had any trouble. . . . She should never have done that at all, even if it was true she shouldn't have said it. [Interviewer: What was the right thing to do?] Well, naturally, what she should have done is stand behind the teacher all the way. Otherwise the teacher loses face with the kids and with the parents and that makes it harder for her to keep order or anything from then on. (Becker, 1953, reprinted, 1970, p. 157)

In this sense, therefore, support was understood in terms of situations where the senior management and classroom teacher interacted on a face-to-face basis: a supportive head would always back up (believe; argue for; help) the teacher.

In addition, classroom teachers also used the term 'support' to refer to less obvious instances of back up, where they believed that the SMT, by their action and inaction, could directly affect discipline in the school.

Visibility and predictability of response
The 'visibility' of the headteacher was a recurrent theme when teachers spoke about their senior staff. Teachers expect the SMT to be 'in touch' with events in the school. Consequently, where the headteacher and her/his SMT colleagues could be seen walking the corridors, visiting lessons and, most importantly, acting against indiscipline, this too was considered to be supportive of classroom teachers:

> the head we have got at the moment is seen around the school far more [than his predecessor]. He takes a much bigger part of his job as being seen around. So he walks the corridors and he'll come into lessons and he talks to pupils far more, comes to assemblies, that sort of thing. [Interviewer: How does that help with discipline?] He can see for himself where there's a difficulty and *he* is seen to deal with the problem, sort it out, if there is one. That makes the pupils aware of him. So I think that's important, I think that the characteristics of the senior

management team are the most important in the school. (M 15/
5 MPG history)

It is revealing that this interviewee emphasized that the headteacher was 'seen to deal with the problem'. The teacher not only
valued the greater visibility of the headteacher *per se*, he also gave
special merit to the fact that *he* (the headteacher) could be *seen*
acting to enforce discipline. Many interviewees stressed the
importance of public action, especially against those who had
committed relatively serious acts of indiscipline. Teachers stressed
not simply the need for action, to punish the individual, but the
need for visible action (to discipline others who witness, or know
of, the school's response):

> One lad was sent out, Friday last week. He'd threatened a
> colleague of mine . . . and he was back in school on Monday
> morning as though nothing had happened – and staff see that
> happening all too often. (M 15/9 MPG+incentive allowance
> personal and social education)

> for everyone's morale, both other pupils, who've been threat-
> ened, and for members of staff it has to be seen that justice has
> been done in some way. (F 20/5 MPG +incentive allowance
> chemistry)

In addition to the requirement that action should be visible,
classroom teachers also argued that the school's response to any
single incident should be consistent with previous cases, i.e. they
sought a predictable response. This returns us to the question of
discretion, which was mentioned earlier: '*To make it clear cut*, so
you'd know that certain things you deal with it this way, certain
other things should be dealt with in another way' (F 2/2 MPG
special needs). During our interviews, classroom teachers placed
great emphasis on the need for consistency. They argued that this
was both fair to pupils and in the interests of staff, who would (a)
know how to react to any act of indiscipline, and (b) be certain that
their actions would carry the weight of established precedents.
Where members of senior staff acted in unusual and, therefore,
unpredictable ways they were likely to anger classroom teachers.
For example:

> there was a case recently where a boy in my class brought a
> knife. He was a first-year and he had only been in school a
> fortnight. He had a knife on him all day; pulled it out at the end
> of the afternoon and did attack some first-year boys with it. He
> didn't actually hurt them but he cut a bag with it, cut with the
> knife. Now to me there should have been some kind of
> suspension, even if it was just for the day. Now that boy was
> taken home by the deputy who saw the parents and explained
> what happened . . . and the boy was then returned to school.

Now I thought that was wrong, and so did a lot of staff here, because there should have been an example made straight away on that day, that that boy was no longer in school because he had brought a knife in. . . . I said to the head, 'Well, can't he stay at home until his parents come in?' But the deputy head had actually been home and seen the parents and they were aware of what was going on. To be honest a lot of staff felt quite strongly about that and when we tried to push it further it was too late. (F 5/5 MPG+incentive allowance English)

This case neatly demonstrates some of the key themes of teacher discourse concerning discipline and the role of senior staff. The case of a first-year who brought a knife to school and used it against other pupils' property was clearly identified as a very serious incident by staff at all levels. Indeed, the deputy headteacher reacted immediately by taking the pupil home and speaking with his parents. It could be argued, therefore, that the deputy had reacted with commendable speed as befits the seriousness of the incident. Yet many teachers were angered that the pupil was allowed back into school so quickly. They were concerned that the school's response had been essentially invisible – 'there should have been an example made straight away on that day, that that boy was no longer in school . . .'.

Openness and shared information
One of the reasons for teachers' anger when justice is not *seen* to be done, relates to the fact that pupils are adept at pointing out apparent inconsistencies in the treatment of offenders. Indeed, there is evidence that pupils favour teachers whose responses to disciplinary issues they perceive as fair, where fairness involves not only the relative severity of response, but also its 'consistency and predictability' (Woods, 1983, pp. 58–9; Gillborn, 1987, pp. 81–4). Where pupils are able to point out 'inconsistencies' in staff's response, teachers feel exposed – it is as if they have somehow lost the support of their colleagues and institution. Similarly, throughout our interviews, teachers stressed the need for SMT to share information concerning incidents and the disciplinary action which had been taken. Where such information was not forthcoming teachers felt exposed and isolated:

A member of my tutor group was involved in [a serious incident recently] – *in some way* – I don't know to what extent but I know that he was suspended for three days. Nobody actually *told* me he was suspended, I wasn't formally told even though he was in my tutor group. I got it on the grapevine from the rest of the tutor group. When he returned he was quite blasé about what h d happened and the first thing he asked me was did I like his suntan? He'd had a three day holiday [i.e. the suspension]. And I found it very difficult to know what to say because I didn't know what his involvement had been, I hadn't been told. Were the police prosecuting him? The police had certainly been involved in tracing those who'd been involved. . . . What was I supposed to do? What was I supposed to say? Was I supposed to wag my finger at him and say, 'You're a naughty boy' or 'Yes, I like your suntan', or 'Don't do it again sonny' – I mean I don't know what I'm supposed to have said, so I said nothing. (F 1/1 MPG modern languages)

Contradictions in teacher discourse

In terms of disciplinary issues, therefore, classroom teachers required their headteacher and management team to fulfil certain expectations. Put simply, SMT should be supportive of classroom teachers. In times of conflict or incident, this meant that SMT should assume that the teacher's account was truthful and that s/he had acted in good faith: more routinely, a supportive management team would respond to acts of indiscipline in ways which were both visible and predictable. Furthermore, teachers expected their SMT to keep them informed of disciplinary happenings – to find out about things from 'the grapevine', or worse still from pupils, was interpreted as a failure of trust and symbolic of the distance between management and staff. Before considering the ways in which management discourse conflicted with such views it is useful to briefly comment on the internal contradictions of the teachers' discourse.

Despite their concern for openness and consistency through colleagues' visible and predictable responses to acts of indiscipline, classroom teachers frequently revealed that they sometimes responded in ways which were neither visible nor predictable. Partly, this arose from an appreciation of the complexity of life in schools. As our original research report showed, for example, when discussing physical aggression from pupils, teachers were careful to emphasize that the *situational context* of an interaction meant that, in most cases, even a physical blow against a member of staff should not be interpreted as an assault (Gillborn *et al.* 1989, pp. 256-9). Similarly, there were occasions where some teachers recognized that backing up a colleague might not always be appropriate:

the accusation was – it was a wrong accusation – but the accusation was that a senior member of staff had not backed up a teacher. That teacher had demanded that a kid took a hat off. The senior teacher said he wasn't prepared to [insist that the pupil] do that. It just so happens that the kid had just got back into school after truanting and would have gone off again had the hat come off, so you know, he said he wouldn't back up the teacher. (M 11/6 MPG+incentive allowance English)

This example is interesting because although the interviewee confirmed that the senior teacher 'said he wouldn't back up the teacher', he rejects the accusation that the SMT member acted incorrectly ('it was a wrong accusation'). Although they are rare, occasions such as this serve to highlight the contradictions and tensions which exist within teacher discourse. A much more common example of such contradiction can be found in teachers' use of personal contacts within the school in preference to the official support system. Rather than moving through the hierarchy and involving different layers of management, according to the seriousness of the incident, many teachers stated that they frequently went to an individual colleague whom they respected and knew would deal with the case in the appropriate way.

Teachers offered a variety of reasons for by-passing the system in this way, including the difficulty of contacting senior staff, especially in split-site schools; the soft disciplinary record of certain SMT members; and the time consuming nature of referral and consultation in some schools. However, the simple constraints of time and workloads frequently led staff to disregard their own ideals concerning the kind of openness, visibility and predictability which they routinely expected of senior staff. As one interviewee put it, 'teachers usually use the channel they think either is easiest or quickest or will work best for them' (F 14/ 5 MPG+incentive allowance mathematics).

MANAGEMENT DISCOURSE

In this section I focus on the views and concerns of headteachers and their senior management teams. Although there are, of course, important differences in the status, roles and responsibilities of different SMT members, they are united by a common concern with administrative duties which take them away from classroom teaching. The National Survey of Teachers in England and Wales (Gray and Sime, 1989), for example, collected data on a nationally representative stratified sample of more than 3,500 primary and secondary teachers. The vast majority of secondary teachers spent most of their contracted time on classroom teaching.[4] In contrast, less than 5 per cent of headteachers and less than 20 per cent of deputies indicated that they spent more than half of their timetable on classroom teaching. In addition, there is evidence that as budget cuts are felt and the pace of educational change increases so the disciplinary and punitive aspects of the management-line relationship become more pronounced (Ball, 1987). In some schools this has already been seen to lead to a greater sense of team identity and responsibili y between SMT colleagues (Gillborn, 1989). It is, therefore, reasonable to conceive of SMT members as a relatively distinct grouping within the secondary school.

The discourse which was characteristic of SMT members was sometimes echoed by staff in middle management positions; including those in positions of responsibility for pastoral and academic matters, such as heads of year and heads of department. However, the majority of middle managers with whom we spoke, especially heads of department, tended to repeat the views and concerns typical of the teacher discourse which I outlined above. As I noted earlier, there can be no all-encompassing definition of the staff who used the teacher and management discourses. In the words of Rizvi and Kemmis (1987, p. 275) my 'aim is not to stereotype either groups or discourses' but to focus on the ways in which language is used in relation to disciplinary issues and present an interpretation of 'the broad distribution of styles of discourse' as they related to participants' structural locations within the school. Hence, in analysing management discourse I am essentially concerned with the ways in which headteachers and SMT members spoke about discipline in their schools. Although there were similarities, in important respects management discourse conflicted with key elements of the teacher discourse.

Management concerns: key concepts in management discourse

Support
The headteachers and deputies we interviewed were usually very much aware of classroom teachers' concern that SMT should be supportive over disciplinary issues. In one school, for example, the headteacher had written a notice, entitled 'courtesy', which was displayed in the staffroom. The notice reaffirmed the head's belief in the need for courtesy and stated that pupils' verbal and physical abuse of teachers, including 'overt or covert sexual inuendo', was a serious matter for which pupils must 'accept the consequences'. The notice continued:

> The offender must be brought to the attention of a senior member of staff who will, if necessary or required, demonstrate his/her disapproval of the actions of the pupil. . . .

> At no times must matters such as the above [e.g. verbal and physical abuse] be ignored. At all times colleagues WILL receive senior staff support. If we ignore or deal badly with any infringement of the bounds of courtesy then we undermine one another. If we do not give mutual support we are all threatened and our supply teachers most of all will face difficulties.

> We will give mutual support to one another. If any colleague is dissatisfied with the level of support given over any particular incident then I should be informed immediately. (The notice was signed by the headteacher)

The head's notice is interesting because it apparently echoes many

of the central concerns of the teacher discourse. First, the word
'support' is very prominent; secondly, staff are assured that 'At all
times colleagues WILL receive senior staff support' (original
emphasis). Indeed, if staff are dissatisfied (i.e. feel unsupported),
the head says that he wants to hear from them. Furthermore, the
notice highlights the staff's collective responsibility, embodying
the teachers' concern with consistency (predictability) in the
identification of and response to indiscipline: 'If we ignore or deal
badly with any infringement . . . then we undermine one another'.
Hence, the notice seems to reflect the complex nature of support,
which was seen to operate both directly (in a face-to-face situation) and indirectly, through the consistent efforts of all staff.

The notion of teachers' collective responsibility also arose
during interviews, where SMT made it clear that support was not
something which they alone could, or should, provide. Teaching
colleagues, especially within subject departments, were seen as an
invaluable resource:

> I don't want teachers who are copies of other teachers, that
> doesn't work. But teachers who seek advice and colleagues who
> offer advice – when its sought – without belittling the teacher
> who has asked for it. It may be physically standing alongside
> them in front of the group of children; it may be a quiet word
> over a cup of coffee. It can be in all sorts of ways. Supporting
> the teacher but not undermining them . . . it really isn't the end
> of the world as long as you've got other colleagues you can turn
> to who will offer support . . . . (M 21/16 deputy)

The notice which I quoted (above) was a particularly clear example
of the ways in which management discourse on disciplinary issues
apparently echoed the teacher discourse. However, it is not
without significance that the notice mentioned, almost in passing,
that SMT would demonstrate their disapproval of the pupil's
actions 'if necessary or required'. Within the context of the notice
the words appear unremarkable. They do, however, offer a clue to
the main point of conflict between the management and teacher
discourses; a conflict which centred upon the teachers' desire for
predictability, and the management's use of 'discretion'.

Discretion: flexibility versus consistency
In their report, *Good behaviour and discipline in schools*, Her Majesty's
Inspectors outlined several areas of 'good practice'. Among nine
'Leadership' items were:

- creating the conditions for *agreement about the standards* to be
  expected and about how they will be achieved;
- seeing to it that such standards are *consistently applied*;
- encouraging *all* teachers to accept responsibility for maintain-

ing good behaviour in the classroom and elsewhere; (HMI, 1989, para. 14: emphasis added)

These requirements are familiar as aspects of support which featured in both teacher and management discourses, especially concerning the need for predictability in teachers' identification of and response to acts of indiscipline. Indeed, throughout the report HMI frequently refer to the need for consistency, a key concept in teacher discourse. However, whilst the HMI document calls for the schools' 'aims and policies' to be 'applied consistently and fairly' (para. 13), it also states that the 'best lists of sanctions . . . insist on *flexibility* in the application of sanctions to suit individual circumstances' (para. 43: emphasis added).

Similarly, the Report of the Committee of Enquiry into Discipline in Schools (The Elton Report) recommended that:

headteachers and teachers should ensure that rules are applied *consistently* by all members of staff, but that there is *flexibility* in the use of punishments to take account of individual circumstances. (Recommendation 25, DES/WO, 1989: emphasis added)

The problem of being simultaneously consistent and flexible is not pursued, or even acknowledged, in either the Elton Report or the HMI document. Yet the problem lay at the heart of a fundamental conflict between teacher and management discourse on discipline. Although both teachers and managers would agree, in principle, with the need for consistency *and* flexibility, in practice – because of their structural location within the school and demands which they faced – teacher discourse overwhelmingly emphasized the need for consistency. Hence, the school's reaction to indiscipline was required to be predictable and visible (see above): if SMT's actions did not fulfil these requirements, they were in danger of being labelled inconsistent and even unsupportive.

In contrast to teacher discourse, managers give much more weight to flexibility. Although they required their staff to be consistent ('At no times must matters such as the above be ignored': the courtesy notice), SMT retained, for themselves, the right to be flexible in their own reading of situations and decisions about appropriate action. SMT saw this not as inconsistency, but as sensitivity and the proper use of discretion. They felt justified in their actions, but were also aware that staff might not understand them:

We attempt to make sure that we as heads and deputies, if you like, the senior team of the school, are not used as the quick line response too often. One way that we deal with that is to say that if you are getting into real difficulties with a pupil, certainly send them up to us and we will hold them. Our preference would be to hand them back, for the teacher to deal with (when they've got a bit more time) or pass them on to the head of faculty or the head of house for them to deal with it. Because it can become too serious in a pupil's mind if it's the head or deputies dealing with it, so what we tend to do is hold them and pass them back. Now there's a danger sometimes that staff will see that as the head and deputies not acting, but there's judgement involved there, whether we feel that the staff needs absolute support instantly and has to be seen to be carried out. Again every case is different. (M 18/2 headteacher)

Some teachers will say that you should treat every case exactly the same. Well, I don't think that's always fair. Sometimes the circumstances are very different and I refuse to punish someone just because that's what the rules say we should do. I try to treat every case on its merits. (M 21/16 deputy)

Earlier, I noted that classroom teachers' concern with visible and predictable responses, and with openness between SMT and staff, could be seen to relate to their day-to-day experience in the classroom where SMT's failure to deliver could leave teachers feeling isolated and exposed. Hence, teacher discourse reflected the particular structural location of staff who spent the majority of their time in classroom teaching situations. Similarly, the particular location and interests of headteachers and senior staff was reflected in the management discourse which simultaneously acknowledged teachers' concerns yet gave equal weight to the need for discretion and flexibility of response.

The greater concern with flexibility in management discourse partly reflects SMTs' belief that they are in a better position to judge the wider complexities of individual cases. Such a position is more easily sustainable for senior management who generally do not spend the majority of their time in classrooms and therefore (some teachers might argue) do not face the immediate consequences of apparent inconsistencies. For example, in commenting on the main disciplinary issues in his school, one headteacher explicitly acknowledged the different perceptions which SMT and classroom teachers might have as a result of their positions and experiences:

probably the main weakness in our system is that it may well be that there are a few kids that we hang on to far too long. And I think that that may well – I don't know, I think that that is more likely to be a staff perception than our perception as a senior staff because they are at the sharp end. (M 19/6 headteacher)

Members of senior management frequently recognized that they were not 'at the sharp end' in terms of discipline. In some of the schools which we visited, for example, there was a general feeling that even when senior management did get involved in classroom teaching, unlike other staff they did not have to 'prove themselves' or 'win' respect, i.e. both classroom teachers and some SMT members believed that the managers' greater power within the institution influenced pupils' actions in their lessons.

These differences between the teacher and management discourses indicate something of the isolation of senior management within schools – an isolation which influences their perception of events and their willingness to use discretion, even where they fear that classroom teachers might not understand.

Isolation

The isolation of senior staff is often given a tangible quality by their physical location within school buildings. In most schools SMT are located in neighbouring rooms which can place them at a significant physical distance from certain areas of the school. One of the schools which we visited, for example, consisted of three separate buildings on a single site. The 'admin. block' housed the senior staff and also included the school's main sports facilities: of the three blocks, this was the only one which did not operate as a pastoral base for pupils. Hence, the atmosphere of the admin. block was quite different to the other areas of the school where pupils could enter and relax together at any time. In that school, the separate location of the SMT was clearly reflected in teacher discourse: staff spoke of not being known 'over in admin', or of sending pupils 'over to admin'.[5] Hence, the management team were not referred to by name or rank, but by their physical location in a different block to the teaching staff.

In addition to the physical isolation which senior management sometimes experience, their roles and responsibilities necessarily create some distance between themselves and other staff. This seems particularly true of headteachers:

> Headteachers don't know what's going on in their schools. I mean, if we're honest about it. We *think* we know everything and we're constantly surprised as we actually walk round the classrooms. (M 22/5 headteacher)

The role and responsibilities of the headteacher necessarily create a distance between head and staff. The headteacher is responsible not only to her/his staff, pupils, governors and local community, s/he is also answerable to the Local Education Authority (LEA). This can cause a conflict of loyalties. Indeed, even where headteachers consciously try to minimize the distance between themselves and the staff, their location and consequent interests within both their school and the wider educational system, act to highlight the 'management-line relationship [which] is at heart disciplinary and punitive' (Ball, 1987, p. 165). This is summed up by one headteacher:

My job is not the most important one in the school by far. . . . Schools are here for children and for staff to teach, and all I do is enable them to do that. So I don't stand on ceremony and I don't believe in creating an autocracy and a power structure – I think we should share our problems; we should share our concerns, and in that way we come to common solutions which enable us to move forward. Now having said all of that, I do believe there has to be a boss in a school, I do believe there has to be a high standard for kids and a high standard for staff, and I'm fairly strict in both fields. The staff know where they stand and if things are not right I shall tell them. (M 24/7 headteacher)

CONCLUSION: CONFLICTS, CONSTRAINTS AND POSSIBILITIES

When classroom teachers and their senior management talk about discipline, they seem to share many of the same concerns, for example, the concept of 'support' is central to both groups. When the language is considered in more detail, however, it becomes apparent that beneath the surface similarities, there lie important contrasts and even conflicts. In fact, when considering disciplinary issues in their schools, classroom teachers and senior management use different discourses: where discourse refers not only to the language used but also the relations between language and the structural location and interests of the speakers, i.e. in the Foucaldian sense (Foulcault, 1977; 1980; Rabinow, 1984) as 'those fields of practice constituted through the interpretation of knowledge and power' (Tyler, 1988, p. 164).

To some degree the contrasts between teacher and management discourses resemble the different perspectives which Keddie (1971) observed in operation among a group of humanities teachers in a London comprehensive. In educationist contexts, such as departmental meetings, the teachers espoused points of progressive educational theory which, for example, rejected notions of innate ability. Once in the teacher context of the classroom, however, the pressures and constraints of the teacher role led them to operate in ways which contradicted their progressive rhetoric. A great deal of work has focused upon the constraining demands of the teacher role, demands which are reflected in the practical orientation of teacher culture (Dale, 1977; Hargreaves, 1980; Poppleton et al., 1987; Sachs and Smith, 1988). Similarly, the data presented in this chapter highlighted a division between teachers and management which both reflected, and was reinforced by, the different location, experiences and interests of two groups.

Classroom teachers' discourse reflected their position 'at the sharp end' of disciplinary matters. As participants who spend the majority of their contracted time in classroom situations the teachers emphasized the importance of consistency, by which they meant that all staff, including senior management, should routinely identify and respond to acts of indiscipline in a predictable and visible way. For classroom teachers 'it has to be seen that justice has been done' (F 20/5 MPG+incentive allowance chemistry). Furthermore, classroom teachers expect their senior management to support them both directly (by backing them up in face-to-face encounters with pupils, parents etc.) and indirectly (by being *open* and sharing information about disciplinary issues). In Keddie's terms, classroom teachers' discourse was dominated by their experiences and concerns within teacher contexts.

Headteachers and other members of schools' senior management teams typically viewed disciplinary issues from a different perspective. They recognized the importance of support to teachers' morale and accepted that this was a major part of their responsibilities. However, management discourse also stressed the collective responsibility to be mutually supportive which applied to all staff. In addition, SMT reserved the right to be flexible in their response to acts of indiscipline: management discourse referred to their sensitivity rather than inconsistency. This position reflected the specific location, roles and responsibilities of managers who were relatively isolated from the day-to-day pressures of the classroom and, hence, were free to sustain a view more in keeping with the educationist context within which they operated.

Given teachers' and managers' contrasting, and sometimes conflicting, emphases upon consistency and flexibility as key concepts in their disciplinary discourses, it is clear that complete agreement (and, therefore, 'absolute' support) may never be possible. The analysis does, however, suggest ways in which progress may be possible, especially concerning the degree of openness which characterizes senior managements' discourse within their own schools. Interviews with classroom teachers, in each of the ten inner-city comprehensives which we visited, pointed to the importance of shared information and a style of management which did not keep teachers 'in the dark'. Where management tried to clearly communicate what was happening, and the reasons for particular SMT actions, teachers were less likely to feel the victims of management whim or weakness. Unfortunately, we must also remember that management–teacher relationships are themselves situated within a constraining educational system which is currently undergoing massive reform. Despite the best efforts of the teaching profession, it may be that the introduction of national assessment and testing linked to a prescriptive National Curriculum may only serve to increase disciplinary problems and widen the gulf between teachers and senior management, especially given the greater administrative burden, and increased SMT isolation within school, which may result from the devolution of financial control under local management of schools.

ACKNOWLEDGEMENTS

I would like to thank all the members of the Quantitative and Qualitative Studies in Education (QQSE) research group for their help and support. Special thanks to the staff and pupils of the ten schools who co-operated with the research project so fully, and to the following friends and colleagues who commented on an earlier draft of this chapter: Wilfred Carr, Dorn Gillborn, John Gray, Jon Nixon, Pam Poppleton, Jean Rudduck and Nicholas Sime.

Correspondence may be addressed to: David Gillborn, QQSE, Educational Research Centre, Arts Tower Floor 9, University of Sheffield, Sheffield S10 2TN, United Kingdom.

NOTES

1. The interview-based research was designed and conducted by Jon Nixon, Jean Rudduck, Gillian Squirrell and myself. The analysis and interpretation in this chapter are, however, solely my responsibility.
2. The following information will be given after each quotation; gender (M/F); years experience teaching (in total/in present school); salary scale (main professional grade/allowance for special responsibility/ deputy/headteacher); main subject specialism. A woman who has been teaching physics for fifteen years, six in her current school, and receives an incentive allowance, would therefore appear as: (F 15/6 MPG+incentive allowance physics).
3. In talking about *teacher* discourse I am emphasizing key elements which frequently emerged in interviews with classroom teachers and which seemed to be related to their shared identity and common experiences. I use the concept as an *ideal type*, i.e. an abstraction from reality for the purposes of analysis – ideal, not in any judgemental sense, but as a simplified construct (a heuristic) to aid analysis and discussion (Weber, 1904).
4. A full breakdown by pay scale and contact time was not published in the original report. I am very grateful to John Gray and Nicholas Sime for allowing me to draw upon the National Survey database in this way. Special thanks to Nicholas Sime for taking the time to prepare the following figures for me:

   Teachers were asked how much of their contracted time was spent on classroom teaching; all or most; well over half; half or less. Contact time varied with teachers' pay scale such that 88 per cent of MPG teachers said they spent all or most of their contracted time on classroom teaching; for those with allowances A or B the figure was 76 per cent. Of teachers on allowances C, D or E, 49 per cent indicated all or most, while 42 per cent ticked well over half. In stark contrast 84 per cent of deputies and 96 per cent of headteachers spent half or less of their contract time on classroom teaching.

5. These quotations are paraphrased to protect the anonymity of interviewees.

REFERENCES

Ball, S J (1987) *The Micro-politics of the School: Towards a Theory of School Organisation*, London: Methuen.

Becker, H S (1951) Role and Career Problems of the Chicago Public School teacher, *Doctoral thesis*, University of Chicago.

Becker, H S (1953) 'The Teacher in the Authority System of the Public School', in Becker, H S (1970) *Sociological Work: Method and Substance*, 1977 edn, New Brunswick: Transaction Books, pp. 151–63.

Connell, R W (1985) *Teachers' Work*, London: George Allen and Unwin.

Dale, R (1977) *The Structural Context of Teaching*, Milton Keynes: Open University Press.

DES/WO (1989) *Discipline in Schools, Report of the Committee of Enquiry chaired by Lord Elton*, London: HMSO.

Earley, P (1989) 'Expectations and Entitlements: Teachers' views of their managers', *Topic: Practical Applications of Research in Education*, Issue 1, Spring.

Foucault, M (1977) *Discipline and Punish: the birth of the Prison*, trans Sheridan, A, Harmondsworth: Penguin.

Foucault, M (1980) *Power/Knowledge: selected interviews and other writings 1972–1977*, ed. Gordon, C., New York: Pantheon Books.

Gillborn, D A (1987) The Negotiation of Educational Opportunity: the final years of compulsory schooling in a multi-ethnic inner-city Comprehensive, *Ph.D. thesis*, University of Nottingham.

Gillborn, D A (1989) 'Talking Heads: reflections on secondary headship at a time of rapid educational change', *School Organisation*, **9**, 1, 65–83.

Gillborn, D A, Nixon, J and Rudduck, J (1989) 'Teachers' Experiences and Perceptions of Discipline in Ten Inner-City Comprehensive Schools', Appendix D, Part II, DES/WO (1989) op cit., pp. 251–77.

Gray, J and Sime, N (1989) 'Findings from the National Survey of Teachers in England and Wales', Appendix D, Part I, DES/WO (1989) op cit., pp. 222–50.

Hargreaves, D H (1980) 'The Occupational Culture of Teachers', in Woods, P (ed.) *Teacher Strategies: Explorations in the Sociology of the School*, London: Croom Helm, pp. 125–48.

HMI (1989) *Education Observed 5: Good behaviour and discipline in schools*, revised reprint, London: HMSO.

Keddie, N. (1971) 'Classroom Knowledge', in Young, M F D (ed.) *Knowledge and Control: New Directions for the Sociology of Education*, London: Collier-Macmillan, pp. 133–60.

Lacey, C (1977) *The Socialization of Teachers*, London: Methuen.

Macdonell, D (1986) *Theories of Discourse: An Introduction*, Oxford: Basil Blackwell.

Poppleton, P, Deas, R, Pullin, R and Thompson, D (1987) 'The Experience of Teaching in "Disadvantaged" Areas in the United Kingdom and the USA', *Comparative Education*, **23**, 3, 303–15.

Rabinow, P (1984) 'Introduction', in Rabinow, P (ed.) *The Foucault Reader*, Harmondsworth: Penguin, pp. 3-29.

Rizvi, F and Kemmis, S with Walker, R, Fisher, J and Parker, Y (1987) *Dilemmas of Reform: An overview of issues and achievements of the Participation and Equity Program in Victorian schools, 1984-1986*, Victoria: Deakin Institute for Studies in Education.

Sachs, J and Smith, R (1988) 'Constructing Teacher Culture', *British Journal of Sociology of Education*, **9**, 4, 423-36.

Tyler, W (1988) *School Organisation: A Sociological Perspective*, London: Croom Helm.

Weber, M (1904) 'The Ideal Type', excerpts from 'Objectivity', Archiv fur Sozialwissenschaft und Sozialpolitik, repr. in Thompson, K and Tunstall, J (eds) (1971) *Sociological Perspectives: selected readings*, Harmondsworth: Penguin, pp. 63-7.

Woods, P (1983) *Sociology and the School: An Interactionist Viewpoint*, London: Routledge and Kegan Paul.

Chapter 3

Teachers and Magistrates Working Together: The School Report

Eileen Baglin Jones

INTRODUCTION

School reports to the courts influence decisions made about the lives of young people and are thus powerful documents. If we look at the historical accounts of the juvenile court in general, and the use of school reports in particular, these show clearly how such reports have become a topic of considerable debate in attitudes towards juvenile justice in the 1980s. The compiling and presentation of reports, and the use made of them by magistrates for purposes of sentencing young people, is a complex issue.

First, there is the process of how School Report Forms are initially designed to be completed by teachers. The pattern across the country varies: some local authorities depend upon their education departments to take a lead, others rely on the social service departments. The forms themselves vary. Some contain detailed questions while others offer a list of general headings. There are also different ways in which different schools go about the task of compiling the reports. Whose task it is, how much consultation is involved and who signs the form, are all further examples of questions dealt with differently in different areas. Some schools use the form to offer the court positive information about a pupil in mitigation of the offence or reason for the court appearance. However, other schools see the form as a way of possibly removing a troublesome pupil from school, and the form is completed with data aimed specifically to bring this about. To this extent the form may be seen by teachers as a way to widen the punishment of pupils, not only for the offence that brings the pupil into court, but for behaviour elsewhere in school where teachers possibly feel they have not had the appropriate sanctions to punish adequately.

It is also true that the school report, in spite of the power it has to influence magistrates about the disposal of cases, is part of a much wider set of legal, cultural, traditional, local community and personal practices, which determine how the juvenile justice system works, in all its variety, in Britain. We have to bear this in mind in looking at one particular, but important, part of this system; the compiling, presentation, and utilization of school reports in the juvenile court.

Since legislation was introduced in 1933, requiring local authorities to provide information about a pupil's record at school, the aim has been that this should be a mitigating exercise in favour of the pupil. Evidence indicates, however, that school court reports can increase the severity of sentences, most probably as a result of teachers submitting information about a pupil which has no direct relevance to circumstances surrounding the offence (Ball, 1981; 1983).

This pioneering work by Ball led to the suggestion that school reports may have a greater influence on courts' decisions than has hitherto been realized. The research also concluded that magistrates had greater confidence in school reports than in others they received. The 1983 research focused on the practice relating to school reports and the issue of confidentiality.

The concern about the way school reports were being used prompted the National Association for the Care and Resettlement of Offenders (NACRO) to publish the results of a NACRO working party in 1984 called *School Reports in the Juvenile Court*. This was followed up in 1988 when a reconvened group of experts reflected on the impact made by the original publication and made further recommendations, looking into what had happened in the period 1984–88. This second publication is called *School Reports in the Juvenile Court: A Second Look* (NACRO, 1988).

The work of NACRO has made a significant contribution to the very limited amount of research which has been carried out in this field. The 1984 Report revealed 'widespread concern and anxiety about procedure and practice' and drew attention to the lack of national guidelines about any aspect of school reports to juvenile courts – procedures, design of forms, need for policies, for example. The fact that 'the school report is a far more important document in the lives of children who appear before the courts than most of those who produce and receive them' was emphasized (NACRO, 1984). The quality of reports, the way in which they are used, the lack of positive remarks about juveniles and the need for in-service training for teachers writing the reports were all flagged as important issues.

Pask (1985) made an interesting point when he suggested that the pastoral system in many schools does not lend itself to the good writing of school reports. His approach as a headteacher was to make improvements in the way reports are dealt with in schools. Parker *et al.* (1987) offered a different solution. They concluded that the content of school reports encouraged a moral assessment of the pupil's character and observed that extremely judgemental and negative comments were being made. They noted that the reports from schools often included examples of hearsay evidence and unsubstantiated allegations. They were in agreement that school reports can be extremely persuasive documents for magistrates and suggested that any pertinent information should be filtered by the writer of the social inquiry report and that school reports for children over the age of 13 be abolished.

It is clear that there are many difficulties associated with preparing school reports connected with the complexity of the system and the confusion of aims. It also appears from the limited research to date that practice is varying regarding the disclosure of reports. This is in spite of the new Children and Young Persons Rules (1988), which followed the recommendations of the NACRO 1984 Working Party and gave parents the right to see reports. There was continuing anxiety expressed in the NACRO 1988 Report that disclosure would not influence the content of school reports and the manner, timing and purpose of disclosure may be at best unhelpful or at worst positively damaging. If the reports are not seen until half an hour before the case is heard, or even in the courtroom itself, this does not give parents, pupils or their legal representatives adequate opportunity to digest, comment upon or question the contents.

A further area of development since 1984 has been the setting up of mechanisms by some local authorities to monitor the impact and outcomes of the local juvenile justice system. These local authorities have used various methods 'to evaluate the impact on policy and practice, to minimize the impact of unintended consequences and to bring about a more just and coherent juvenile justice system locally' (NACRO, 1988). Evidence collected by NACRO's Juvenile Crime Section suggests that systematic examination of the impact of school court reports does not take place. This compounds the problems considered in this chapter.

In early 1986, the issues discussed above regarding school court reports, did not seem to be uppermost in the minds of teachers writing the court reports for a petty sessional division in Oxfordshire – the subject of this chapter. The reports which were being received from schools seemed slight, sometimes biased and generally unsatisfactory. They could certainly not be seen as helpful to the juveniles who appeared before the magistrates. Discussion among magistrates revealed an anxiety that everyone concerned with the production and use of the schools court reports should have thought carefully about them and the need to improve the standard of reporting. This led to the suggestion that a newly-designed School Court Report Form might encourage that better standard. An open meeting was held in April 1986 to which everyone involved in the production and use of school reports was invited. The ideas and issues that came from this meeting resulted in the establishment of a working party to design a new School

Report Form. This new form was piloted by the LEA and the social services department in 1987 in the identified Petty Sessional Division and has subsequently been adopted throughout the County of Oxfordshire.

In this chapter I want first to examine the nature and value of the school court report forms that were used prior to 1986, then describe the collaboration between those concerned, and finally the considerations taken into account in the designing of a new form. The investigation into the School Court Report Form revealed something about what kind of form, and what procedures connected with its preparation and use, are most conducive towards placing balanced and relevant information before magistrates.

Before turning to the detail of our work in Oxfordshire, however, it will be useful to consider briefly the statutory framework for school reports, the conflict between justice and welfare within the juvenile system and the framework for social inquiry for the courts. These are all elements of the landscape against which school reports to the juvenile court have to be seen.

THE STATUTORY FRAMEWORK FOR SCHOOL REPORTS

The production and use of school reports in juvenile courts is controlled by legislation. In 1908 provision was made which separated juveniles from adults within the law. Since then there have been relatively few pieces of legislation which have concerned themselves specifically with juvenile justice. Of these the 1933 Rules and the 1970 Amendments have prescribed the legal framework within which school court reports should be produced and presented. Some significant changes occurred after August 1st 1988 when a new set of Rules came into force.

Rule 10 refers to the production and use of reports from schools. There has been contention about Rule 10 1 (b), which directs magistrates to take into consideration such information as to the general conduct, home surroundings, school record and medical history of the child or young person as may be necessary to enable them to deal with the case in his best interests. Thus, information from school is to be considered alongside other kinds of information. But how this shall be done, how the information should be presented and by whom, are not specified by the Rule and it is easy to understand how confusion has arisen.

Rule 10 ii (a) of the 1970 Rules caused the greatest anxiety and it is this part of the Rules which was changed most significantly by the new Rules. Until 1988 the young offender and the parent or guardian had no right to see the whole report – although they did, ironically, have the right to dispute its claims when they had been told about them. The case could be adjourned for the writer of the report to be compelled to attend the next hearing. Ball's (1983) research suggested that School Court Reports were frequently considered confidential to the court and were not even made available to legal representatives.

In spite of the new obligations for reports to be shared, the questions of confidentiality raised were, and continue to be, vexed and complicated. These are central questions in the debate about the whole matter of School Court Reports. It is important to notice that there has never been a legal test of exactly what Rule 10 means, perhaps partly because it refers to 'local authorities' and not 'local education authorities'. It can, therefore, be interpreted as not applying to school reports. In addition, terms are not clearly defined. Is there a difference, for example, between 'the school record' and 'school report'? Such ambiguity throughout Rule 10, together with the debate which questions whether open reporting leads to better or worse reports in any case, have caused great difficulties to all concerned. When school reports were not open to challenge this seemed to many to represent a denial of natural justice to the young person concerned (Ball, 1983; Scott, 1986; NACRO, 1984) and led to a revision with effect from 1st August 1988.

Rule 10 ii now states that a court shall arrange for copies of any written report before the court to be made available to (a) the legal representative, if any, of the child or young person; (b) any parent or guardian of the child or young person who is present at the hearing; and (c) the child or young person. The exception is where the court otherwise directs on the ground that it appears to it impracticable to disclose the report having regard to the age and understanding of the child or young person, or it is undesirable to do so having regard to serious harm which may thereby be suffered by him.

This Rule brings into effect an important change in the law concerning School Court Reports although it does not remove many of the anxieties alluded to earlier.

JUSTICE OR WELFARE

The dilemma in juvenile justice in England and Wales is that the courts are operating two legal models: the justice model and the welfare model. Up to the 1950s juvenile courts were criminal courts, emphasizing concepts of crime, responsibility and punishment, and juveniles were generally seen as 'bad'. Referred to as 'juvenile delinquents' or 'young offenders' (Molony, 1927; Ferguson, 1952; Emerson, 1969) the emphasis was on determining guilt and imposing punishment.

During the 1960s, influenced by left-wing aspirations and a

quest for social justice (Parker, *et al.*, 1981), the social welfare *treatment* approach was grafted onto the juvenile court structure. This principle of welfare was exemplified as an approach based on assessment, prevention and treatment. The ideas underlying welfare in the state are derived from many sources (Robson, 1976) but the continuing confusion of attempting to run juvenile justice according to both the welfare and justice models is an important factor to be borne in mind when considering the question of school reports to courts. Discussion of this problem can be found in various places. Taylor, *et al.*, (1979) criticized social workers' unfettered intervention in the lives of young offenders in the name of welfare. Floud (1970) points out the tension between a juvenile court which is looking at the needs and interests of the individual and also upholding the values/cultural norms of society. Morris, *et al.*, (1980); Parker *et al.*, (1981) and Davies (1974) all address the problem.

This major difficulty, combined with the diversity of practice in juvenile courts regarding procedure, presentation and use of reports and sentencing (Ball, 1983; Burney, 1979; Parker, *et al.*, 1987) forms the general background against which the question of school reports must be discussed.

SOCIAL INQUIRY FOR THE COURTS

School reports are one part of social inquiry reports. These are written reports, concerned with an individual offender. They are written by members of agencies which have varying independence in court, and they are presented in court and read by magistrates before sentence is announced.

Davies (1974) draws attention to the steady growth of inquiry work in all courts since the 1950s, accompanying the growth of the probation service whose representatives 'have consistently campaigned for an extension of court practice in calling for social inquiry reports'. The Streatfield Report (1961) discussed the positive value of basing a sentence 'on comprehensive and reliable information which is relevant to the objectives in the Court's mind' and this strongly influenced practice in criminal courts. Since the 1960s professional commentators from the Probation Service, the magistracy and criminologists, have agreed that when there is more comprehensive information available about the offender's social background this will lead to more appropriate sentencing and thus increase the effectiveness of the court's decision. During the 1960s courts increasingly came to view the offender as an individual in need of treatment. The old order of deterrence and retribution was existing at this point alongside a newer pattern of individualized measures.

Davies (1974) criticized this as a dual system of sentencing in the adult court. He suggested that it has led to what he called a closed-loop system of influence, with probation officers offering magistrates sentencing options which they expect and are expected to follow. It is, however, the system which applies in the juvenile court. Here magistrates in general do not use tariff sentencing but rely heavily on the contents of the reports they receive to determine the disposal. The reports are therefore 'of very great importance to the juvenile and his [sic] parents' (Cavenagh, 1976). It is difficult to discuss this area without confusion of terminology. 'Social Inquiry Report' is the term used to describe both the whole collection of reports presented and the particular report among those, written by the probation officer or social worker.

CONTENT AND PRESENTATION OF SOCIAL INQUIRY REPORTS

Very little has been written about what should go into a social inquiry report and how it should be written (Perry, 1979). In the absence of particular information about juvenile court reports we can perhaps assume that probation officers and social workers will base their underlying approaches to report writing to both juvenile and adult courts on the same principles. These were originally set down by the Streatfield Report which legitimized pre-sentence reporting: 'The cardinal principle is that a sentence should be based on comprehensive and reliable information which is relevant to objectives in the court's mind' (1981, Para. 341, p.96) and it lists the kind of information which can be included:

- essential details of the offender's home surroundings;
- family background;
- his [sic] attitude to his family and their response to him;
- his school and work record and spare-time activities;
- his attitude to his employment;
- his attitude to the present offence;
- his attitude and response to previous forms of treatment following any previous convictions;
- detailed histories about relevant physical and mental conditions;
- an assessment of personality and character.

(Para. 336:95)

These categories are far from precise: probation officers and social workers find difficulties in meeting the requirements of writing social inquiry reports within such a generalized framework. Areas which potentially cause problems are the lack of expertise in making attitudinal assessments, the differences between report writers, a lack of standardized presentation which makes it impossible to make comparisons, and the presence of too many variables in report writing i.e. information given, sought, presented and received. Perry (1979) expresses anxiety about the declining involvement of probation officers in juvenile courts and questions whether social workers have expertise or time to write appropriate reports.

Such anxieties would be countered by an insistence from many of the report writers and those responsible, that this is a duty which is taken seriously and that, for example 'all probation officers are aware of the great importance of their reports' (McLean, 1961). The influence of social inquiry reports, and the responsibility this places on writers, led to the publication of the DHSS (1987) *Guidelines for Report Writers*. But the guidelines do not refer especially to school reports and none of the social workers interviewed in connection with the new Oxfordshire Form had seen this document. It was not available at any of three social services departments where enquiries were made. Priestly, *et al.*, (1977) suggested that because there is no supervision of content, presentation or recommendations of reports this leads to uneven or inconsistent quality. He also questioned whether the ethics of social work to recognize the value and dignity of every human being, irrespective of origin, status, sex, age, belief or contribution to society (British Association of Social Workers, 1975) may be difficult to reconcile with the function of the court, which is to protect society against crime.

Following the 1969 Children and Young Person's Act local authorities took over responsibility for juvenile enquiries. Thus, unless a juvenile is already being supervised by a probation officer, or is over the age of 16 when social inquiry reports are requested, it is the responsibility of the social services department in liaison with the LEA, to produce them. In practice this means that a school report is requested by the social services department as an administrative exercise and that a social worker will be assigned to the juvenile if one is not already working with the youngster. The social inquiry report may also include a report from an education psychologist, staff of a tutorial unit, a doctor, or an education social worker. The social inquiry report seeks to provide the background information necessary to enable the court to deal appropriately with the juvenile in court (Cavenagh, 1976). It is usual for the social worker or probation officer in their particular report to examine sentencing alternatives and to make recommendations to the court about an appropriate disposal.

SCHOOL REPORTS TO AN OXFORDSHIRE JUVENILE COURT

In the Petty Sessional Division referred to in this chapter there had been some disquiet expressed over a number of years about the way the School Court Report Forms were completed. Attention to this matter was focused at a number of Bench Meetings and a number of issues were identified:

1. The very limited amount of information contained in some of the reports.

For example, one school reported that the pupil concerned has only attended for 87 out of a possible 114 sessions during a three month period. The comments added to this piece of factual information were:

(a) 'he has been with us for only one term so we are unable to comment with any reliability'; and in relation to the absence from school
(b) 'we are unable to state with any confidence but we believe his desire to stay with his local peers was stronger than his wish to return to school'.

Other issues included:

2. the possibility that the bench would be unfair to juveniles because of the information it received;
3. the magistrates were not receiving the right kind of information and thus not enough help in making decisions;
4. some information appeared to be biased and the tone of some reports questionable – being condemnatory and negative;
5. whether schools realized the importance of their reports to the court;
6. the possibility that teachers did not have enough time to complete the reports because of the manner in which some were completed;
7. although usually signed by the headteacher it was felt that the report had not actually been written by the headteacher.

This list of anxieties and problems also seemed to indicate a lack of understanding and poor liaison between the various agencies concerned. A meeting was held which included all magistrates, the Clerk and his deputy, the area social services director and the juvenile court social worker, two probation officers and the headteachers of the five schools within the Petty Sessional Division. The Clerk's letter of invitation to the headteachers, following a preliminary telephone call to discuss suitable dates, said:

The purpose of the meeting will principally be to discuss the provision of school reports to Juvenile Courts. The Magistrates would like to know your views on such matters as the method of provision, the format, confidentiality and perhaps most importantly, how your reports should be interpreted and what weight should be placed upon them. The Chairman has also asked me to invite you to raise any other matter you consider appropriate; it would be helpful to have advance notice of other topics.

This meeting was a landmark: genuine concerns were voiced by all present and the issues were clarified. They seemed to focus on procedures and questions of confidentiality: how the reports were written and obtained and the format of reports; of interpretation – of schools giving opinions as well as facts, and of what kind of information is important, relevant and valuable; who in school is best qualified to write reports?; parental involvement and the role of social workers.

The Magistrates and their Clerk were able to outline the legal procedure, and the problems for magistrates in deciding how to interpret the rules were made clear. As Social Workers and teachers described their difficulties, emphasis was laid on the need for answers to be found jointly.

The meeting was useful as a contact between all parties involved and it seemed to encourage a more positive approach from teachers, making them more aware of what was expected. It raised awareness at that particular time and went some way towards improving communications. There was a unanimous suggestion that the School Court Report Form itself should be reviewed and changed in order to improve the quality of the information and comment it gave. At this meeting the senior social worker revealed that the form was only used in the Petty Sessional Division and different areas of the county used different forms.

A small working party composed of three senior magistrates, two teachers and the Clerk met to consider recommendations made by various people who had been at the earlier meeting and including the educational social workers who for some unaccountable reason had not been invited to take part then. It was perhaps a comment on the very minor role they had hitherto taken in the production of School Court Reports. A new format was agreed by the working party, a mock-up prepared by the Clerk and circulated and then with further amendments, approved for use during a trial period of a year.

It would be possible to discuss in great detail each change or innovation related to the form. However for our purposes here it seems sufficient to indicate the main alterations made and the reasons for them because they reveal the issues considered to be of greatest importance by the people concerned. Of particular importance were the issues of confidentiality, the need for specific and positive information, the role the School Court Report had in deciding the outcome of a court appearance, and matters relating to attendance.

Confidentiality

The issue of confidentiality appeared to produce conflicting views. Some magistrates and at least one headteacher had felt that 'it would be better not to show the report to the juvenile concerned'. The knowledge that this was to happen inhibited the teacher when writing the report for several reasons, not least of these was that the juvenile was likely to return to the same school and the same teachers. This was a view that came from a magistrate who also urged a limited distribution of the reports, 'in the interests of the juvenile concerned, especially where that interest is to try and improve that juvenile's conduct and responsibility in the same environment'. It is perhaps ironic that the same consideration, i.e. the interest of the juvenile concerned, was the one which persuaded the working party to take the opposite view and to urge full and careful discussion of the report between the writer and the juvenile and his/her parents. Some of the unsatisfactory aspects of the juvenile justice system have been outlined but there remains the dilemma of care or control, each aspect being based on a different set of ideas. It still seems important, however, that the discussions about how to share the contents of a court report – when and with what purposes – should remain at the forefront of teachers' minds. There are other issues here of taking responsibility for the report, of using it creatively, of relationships between home and school/pupil and school which some participants in these discussions understood more fully as a result of this piece of work. There are other people, one suspects, less influenced by the discussions and for whom the confidentiality issues remain only partially understood. Enquiries made during court hearings about discussions focusing on the school reports seem to reveal patchy practice.

Nevertheless, these were positive steps taken with the acceptance that reports should, if at all possible, be the subject of home/school discussion before presentation to the juvenile court. Also recognition by the working party that the question of confidentiality was closely connected to decisions about interpretation and of what kind of information is important and valuable.

Positive information

There was considerable discussion about the need felt by magistrates to receive specific and positive information and the difficulties schools seemed to find in providing it. The new form would request more positive information in a very clear way, giving unambiguous requests to schools and stressing clearly the reasons why magistrates needed background information from schools. In line with this the general principles guiding the design of the form would aim to make it possible to elicit the best information available. It needed to be simply presented and designed (one folded A3 sheet – no loose leaves – was agreed upon); unpretentious in its language, easy to read with clear printing and containing several indications of the attitudes and expectations of the magistrates.

Place of the School Court Report in the court proceedings

It was agreed that the importance of the school report in the proceedings would be stressed: 'The magistrates regard the information revealed in School Court Reports as being extremely valuable in assisting them in their determinations'. This sentence was included in the condensed and simplified Introduction to the form which made clear that although it hoped to give adequate guidance to schools, the form should not be so prescriptive that there would be no freedom to give information felt by the school to be important but not specifically asked for. The simple, non-legal language made a strong plea to teachers to fill in the School Court Report Form thoughtfully and usefully, to give reasons for their responses and to regard it as a powerful tool in the hands of the court.

Questions on attendance

The questions about attendance were changed. In the past poor attendance could, it seemed, become such a focus that the juvenile would be in danger of being punished not only for the original offence but for bad attendance as well. By offering the opportunity to comment on this aspect of the pupil's performance at school ('Is attendance at school a problem? – If yes, why?) the pilot form sought to reassure teachers that only relevant information was important. Also, that unnecessary administration of quoting attendance figures for the previous term was not being asked of them.

Apart from these central issues a number of minor matters were considered and other relatively small changes were made to the School Court Report Form. The overall effect was to emphasize the 'care' function of the juvenile court rather than the 'control' function and to make small but significant shifts in the tone and character of the form. The aim was to create the kind of open instrument which schools would find helpful in making a report on pupils as positive as possible.

TOWARDS A NEW SCHOOL COURT REPORT FORM

The pilot stage ran its course without hindrance. In February 1987 a meeting was held to review the use of the new form. There were particular anxieties because there had been a great reduction in the number of juveniles appearing before the court due to the extension of the cautioning policy of the Thames Valley Police. Concern was expressed lest the few forms used would result in bad justice (because magistrates were inexperienced in using School Court Reports) or bad use of forms (because teachers had so few to fill in).

Nevertheless, at the *review meeting* there was a very positive feeling about the wish to co-operate and everyone present 'felt that the form was an improvement upon the old one'. The Chairman led a step-by-step consideration of each question and one or two minor but important amendments were made. For example, on the Introduction to the report the final sentence in the last paragraph was changed from 'The school should therefore consider, whenever possible, consulting the child and/or parents' to 'The school should therefore, whenever practicable, consult . . .'. This betrays a significant change of attitude amongst the people present with the acceptance that the reports should be open documents. This was before the 1988 amendment of the Magistrates' Court Rules had been announced. The decision to make this change to positively encourage the adoption of a consultative approach, was not made without lengthy discussion.

The other amendment was also concerning consultation with parents and children. The minutes record:

> It was accepted that on occasions schools would not wish or would not be able to discuss the report. For example, because information harmful to the child's well-being was included or simply because of lack of time. It would be helpful to the magistrates to know why and for explanation to be given.

The wording of the question was changed to allow an explanation to be given.

It is significant that confidentiality has been a continuous preoccupation at the various stages of development of the form. The review meeting, however, did not just talk about the format of the School Court Report Form and make amendments to it. In exactly the way that the NACRO working party, reconvened in 1988, turned its attention away from the ideal School Court Report Format to a consideration of policies, so this small group spent more time discussing issues, practice and processes.

The involvement of the education social worker was discussed. Few forms in either the pilot year (1987) or in 1986 had included comments from the education social worker. The agreement that social services department should send a separate notification to the education social worker at the same time as the School Court Report was sent to the school seemed to mark a very positive step forward in the inter-agency liaison.

The education social worker had declared that there was poor liaison between social services and education social workers: 'They don't ever refer anything to us'. In 1988 when the separate notification system was working he said 'Things have been going much more smoothly recently. I think the notification only happens in this area – but that has certainly improved things.'

The shortness of time between the receipt by schools of the form and the court hearing was seen as a serious problem during the review meetings. 'The saving of even a few days might well improve the quality of the observations made and give greater opportunity for consultation' (minutes of meeting held on 24th February). The Justice's Clerk agreed to ask the police to consider attaching the notices to the social services department to the summons sets when they are sent to the Clerk for issue. If that were done he could send the notices direct to the social services department. Interestingly, lack of time to complete School Court Report Forms was not perceived as a major problem amongst the teachers interviewed, but the willingness of the Clerk and the social services department to ask the police to co-operate in trying out a new system is an interesting example of the atmosphere of co-operation which this exercise seems to have created.

CONCLUSION

This chapter focuses on the use of a School Court Report Form in one juvenile court, placing it in the wider context of juvenile justice in England and Wales. Some of the unsatisfactory aspects of the juvenile justice system have been outlined, with the continuing dilemma between care and control, and the system based on two quite different sets of ideas. Apart from this difficulty several additional factors are also important: for example, lack of clarity about who has the responsibility for preparing reports for court; and lack of precision in the Rules which has resulted in the development of fragmented local systems – different practice in different areas of the country. As long as there is lack of government policy and co-ordination about School Court Reports the system is likely to remain less than satisfactory. Until radical reform of the kind suggested by the NACRO Report (1988) takes place and school reports, of the kind presently used, are dispensed with, it seems important that local systems must be made effective and current practice should be improved.

In itself, a new form does not necessarily encourage a better standard of reporting. However, the processes of change have provided an opportunity for those concerned to reappraise their attitudes and identify their principles. Some changes in behaviour can already be detected as principles begin to be translated into practice, and the new School Court Report Form was introduced on a countywide basis from 1989. The design and planning of a new School Court Report Form may have greater justification as a planned interim strategy than as an enduring modification to court practice. By encouraging systematic thought about the issues connected with preparing court reports it can act as an important stage in development.

Those involved with the new School Court Report Form have accepted that it is a better form than its predecessor, but analysis has shown that there remains a problem of balanced reporting since its introduction. One reason for this may be the teachers' lack of experience, some of whom showed a lack of understanding of the issues involved. Better ways could be found for teachers to provide background information on juveniles appearing in court by holding discussions with social workers, probation officers or education social workers (rather in the nature of a case conference) and representing the school's point of view through the School Court Report Form. A teacher from the offender's school could actually appear in court and this should not be too difficult to arrange in a compact Petty Sessional Division such as the area studied in this chapter.

The concept of the effective school is an elusive one but to procure balanced and relevant School Court Reports there is a need for effective schools with the kind of pastoral organization which allows them to be objective and make fair judgements about their pupils, even the difficult ones. The court appearance should be part of a wider pastoral process of working with a pupil. Preparation for court, the home–school partnership, and follow-up discussions arising from a court appearance could all be important. Appearing in the juvenile court can be a point in time when a youngster begins on a path of crime, or alternatively the appearance can help to prevent this happening. Sensitive pastoral support from schools has an important part to play. Better schools would mean better relationships which should mean better reports. Changing attitudes can be a lengthy process, but providing opportunities to raise awareness and consider the issues is an important first step as this study has shown. The issues of juvenile justice need to be featured in in-service training for teachers and discussions by others involved. The study has shown that there is a need for training at a more practical level too, to ensure that accurate and complete information is presented by the schools: this has important resource implications for the local authority.

It is important to find ways of checking that the kind of gap between the rhetoric of stated intentions and the reality of practice does not occur: a local monitoring scheme may be possible through improved inter-agency liaison. Differences in perspectives between the various services will demand greater trust, and more time and discussion. This could improve communication and ensure more accurate interpretation of information. Magistrates for example, need to understand school systems and structures and the context from which school reports (of whatever kind) come. The difference between fact and opinion needs to be clearly appreciated and the establishment of a forum where relevant issues can be raised and a fairer standard of reporting be promoted would seem very useful.

Other conclusions concern the kind of School Court Report Form, procedures connected with its preparation, and the best way of placing balanced relevant information before magistrates. The new School Court Report Form can provide magistrates with all the information they need. A structured format, with detailed questions can greatly assist in obtaining a range of information. The changes made to the pre-1987 form were useful in extending its possible scope. There needs to be a balance between adequate information and the inclusion of irrelevant material; a shared definition of what the School Court Report is for; exactly what is wanted; what is the distinctive contribution of the report; its role and function; and the role of the head, or whoever checks the report. The report should be up to date. If the case becomes delayed by court procedures the possibility of a shorter, additional report from school to register any changes should be considered. These aspects should be discussed and their importance understood by all concerned. An understanding of the content and purpose of the School Court Report Form will inform and improve the way in which it is prepared and used.

The question of consultation has been discussed, with reference to the changes in Rule 10 of the Magistrates (CYP) Rules (1988). If School Court Reports are simply handed over in court there could be even more damaging effects than before the Rules changed. Proper time should be given before the court sitting, to a discussion of the reports. Such improvements to practice and procedure are likely if they are encouraged in tandem with wider discussions.

The writing and usage of School Court Reports is difficult: much information is unquantifiable, delicate and depends on relationships. Positive attitudes towards pupils from schools can influence behaviour and change it for the better. If writing a school report is seen as a positive learning experience, it can be an agent for change. Research has shown that the way a child is handled and the demands made on him or her influence his/her behaviour (Rutter et al., 1970). The situation which a youngster is in, the people involved and the nature of the relationship, are all major factors in a child's behaviour. This chapter concludes that the design, production and use of School Court Reports can be an active process. Instead of denying true justice to juveniles the School Court Report Forms can be important tools in building a fair system for all who appear in the juvenile courts.

REFERENCES

Ball, C (1981) 'The Use and Significance of School Reports in Juvenile

Court Criminal Proceedings: a Research Note', *British Journal of Social Work* **11**, pp 479–83.

Ball, C (1983) 'Secret Justice: The Use Made of School Reports in the Juvenile Court', *British Journal of Social Work*, **3**, pp 21–37.

British Association of Social Workers (1975) *Code of Ethics*, London: BASW.

Burney, E (1979) *Magistrate, Court and Community*, London: Hutchinson.

Cavenagh, EW (1976) *Guide to Procedure in the Juvenile Court*, Chichester: Barry Rose.

Children and Young Persons' Act (1933), (Amended 1963), London: HMSO.

Children and Young Persons' Act (1969) London: HMSO.

Criminal Justice Act (1982) London: HMSO.

Davies, M (1974) 'Social inquiry for the courts: an examination of the current position in England and Wales', *British Journal of Criminology*, **14**, 1, January.

Department of Health and Social Security (1987) *Reports to Courts: Practice Guidance for Social Workers*, London: HMSO.

Emerson, R (1969) *Judging Delinquents (Part II)*, Chicago: Aldine Press.

Ferguson, T (1952) *The Young Delinquent in his Social Setting*, Oxford: Oxford University Press.

Floud, J (1970) 'Social class factors in educational achievement', in Craft, M (ed.) *Family Class and Education*, London: Longman.

Magistrates' Courts (1970) (Children and Young Persons) Rules. Ammended 1988.

McLean, DS (1961) 'Probation Reports', *Probation*, **9**, 176–7.

Molony Report (1927) *Committee on the Treatment of Young Offenders*, London: HMSO.

Morris, A, Giller, H, Geach, H and Szwed, E (1980) *Justice for Children*, London: Macmillan.

National Association for the Care and Resettlement of Offenders (1984) *School Reports in the Juvenile Court*, London: NACRO.

National Association for the Care and Resettlement of Offenders (1988) *School Reports in the Juvenile Court: A second look*, London: NACRO.

Parker, H, Casburn, M, Turnbull, D (1981) *Receiving Juvenile Justice*, Oxford: Blackwell.

Parker, H, Sumner, M and Jarvis, G (1987) 'Ill-mannered and lacking in discipline: school reports in the juvenile court', *Youth Social Work*, No. 5, November.

Pask, R (1985) 'Open justice for young offenders', *Education*, May 24th.

Perry, FG (1979) *Reports for Criminal Courts*, London: Owen Wells.

Priestly, P, Fears, D and Fuller, R (1977) *Justice for Juveniles*, London: Routledge and Kegan Paul.

Robson, WA (1976) *Welfare State and Welfare Society: Illusion and Reality*, London: Allen and Unwin.

Rutter, M, Tizard, J and Whitmore, K (eds) (1970) *Education, Health and Behaviour*, London: Longman.

Scott, T (1986) *School Reports for the Juvenile Court* Unpublished Thesis, Oxford University Dept. of Educational Studies.

Streatfield Report (1961) *Pre-sentence Reporting*, London: HMSO.

Taylor, C, Lacey, R and Bracken, D (1979) *In Whose Best Interests?*, London: Cobden Trust/Mind.

Part Two: The Bullying Aspect of Pupil Behaviour

Chapter 4

Bullying: A Whole-School Response

Delwyn Tattum and Eva Tattum

INTRODUCTION

Bullying is the most malicious and malevolent form of deviant behaviour present and widely practised in our schools, yet it has until recently received only scant attention from the education community. As pupils, teachers or parents we have experienced or witnessed it, however, and in fact, research evidence indicates that it is more prevalent and damaging to children than most adults think. The perpetrators are to be found in nursery classes, infant, junior and secondary schools, and their conduct includes name-calling and teasing; jostling and punching; intimidation and extortion; and even assault, maiming and murder. The victims for their part suffer physical and psychological abuse, isolation and loneliness, insecurity, and anxiety arising from the threatening atmosphere which surrounds them. At its most insidious it focuses on vulnerable children who are regarded as being different because of their ethnic origins, homosexual inclinations or physical or mental disabilities.

Bullying also affects those other children who may witness the violence and aggression – and the consequent distress of the victim – and less aggressive pupils can be drawn into the taunting and tormenting of victims by group pressure and other social psychological factors. They too know how quickly the direction of the attack can change, for it is impossible to intimidate and oppress one person without making others afraid. Bullying can adversely affect the atmosphere of a class or even the climate of a school. Children have a basic right to freedom from pain, humiliation and fear, whether caused by adults or other children. Schools have a responsibility to create a secure and safe environment for children in their care so that parents may hand their children over

in the confident knowledge that they will be protected from
bullies.

To conclude this introductory section on our apparent neglect
of the problem at a national level we may examine the recently
published Elton Report on 'Discipline in Schools' (DES, 1989).
This substantial document makes 138 recommendations on discipline but only four address the matter of bullying. The bulk of the
report is concerned with disruptive behaviour and pupil assaults
on teachers, yet its general findings are that assaults on teachers
were infrequent – only 2 per cent reported acts of physical
aggression towards them. In fact, it was lesser misdemeanours
such as chattering, calling out and interfering with other pupils'
work which were the most prevalent and were found to be a
constant drain on teachers' energies and patience. Much of what is
contained in the Elton Report is eminently sensible and balanced,
but one major criticism must be that it failed to seriously address
the problem of acts of aggression and violence by one pupil on
another.

The Report does provide us with valuable data on the extent of
the problem and, of equal importance, teachers' awareness of
bullying in their classrooms and about the school. In order that we
may have baseline data on primary and secondary school teachers'
routine experiences of discipline the Committee commissioned
Sheffield University's Educational Research Centre to conduct a
survey. A stratified random sample of schools was selected to be
statistically representative of the regions and different types of
schools in England and Wales. A questionnaire was sent to the
teachers during early October 1988, asking them to identify from
a prepared list the different types of pupil behaviour they had to
deal with the previous week. There were separate lists for
classroom and about school behaviour. Table 4.1 combines data
extracted from the Report (Tables 1, 2, 9 and 10) which deal
specifically with bullying. From the table it is evident that bullying
is widespread in our schools and that teachers are aware of its
nature and incidence – thus challenging the myth that bullying is a
secretive activity and that is why teachers have not tackled it in a
concerted way. Particularly interesting are the figures relating to
teachers' perceptions of bullying in their classrooms – both verbal
and physical. These figures confirm the findings of Stephenson
and Smith (Tattum and Lane, 1989), who conducted a survey of
teachers and final year primary school children in 26 schools in
Cleveland. As part of their studies they also asked the teachers
and 143 children in the top two year groups in one primary school
to nominate which pupils in their class were bullies and which
were victims. They received a high level of agreement between
the nominations made by teachers and children as to which pupils
were involved in bullying (correlation = .8). Olweus (1978) also

Table 4.1 The Elton Report: Sheffield University Survey
Bullying behaviour at least once during the survey week (October 1988)

Primary School Teachers (n=1200)		
Types of bullying behaviour towards other pupils	In class (%)	About school (%)
Physical assaults: e.g. pushing, punching, striking	74	86
Verbal abuse: e.g. offensive or insulting remarks	55	71

Secondary School Teachers (n=3200)		
Types of bullying behaviour towards other pupils	In class (%)	About school (%)
Physical assaults: e.g. Pushing, punching, striking	42	66
Verbal abuse: e.g. offensive or insulting remarks	62	76

reported high levels of agreement between the nominations made by children of this age and their teachers.

The 'about school' figures are disturbingly high in both primary and secondary schools, especially as we are only dealing with the more overt forms of bullying. Other more subtle and insidious forms of bullying will be discussed in a later section. Maybe it is because teachers are so aware of bullying that they tend to regard it as an inevitable part of school life. Such an attitude is unacceptable for it gives the impression, however misplaced, that schools condone aggression and the domination of one pupil by another. Children have a right to an education in a safe, secure learning environment and adults have a responsibility to provide it.

GROWING INTERNATIONAL AWARENESS AND CONCERN

Despite the fact that bullying is widespread and persistent in schools it is only very recently that the problem has been taken seriously at an international level.

Japan, in its legislation to reform their education system, has an entire section on 'Dealing with School Bullying' in the Second Report on Education Reform (April, 1986). This action follows reports that bullying in Japan caused at least nine student suicides in 1985, as well as several other cases in which victims murdered their tormentors. The Japanese word for bullying is *Ijime* and in a country which takes its education very seriously there is growing concern about the bullying of students by teachers.

The problem has also commanded attention in the United States where a Schoolyard Bully Practicum was held in May 1987 at Harvard University. The Americans are at present embarked on a national programme funded by the Departments of Education and Justice. Their action was prompted by a number of events, none more tragic than the case of 12 year old Nathan Faris from Missouri who was a bright, slightly overweight boy who hated school. He was teased and called names like 'Chubby' and 'Walking Dictionary'. One day he could tolerate it no longer, so he took a gun to class and after fatally wounding a classmate shot himself. Other victims have taken a different course of action, one that puts legal pressure on the school system itself, through taking out lawsuits against the school administrative district. Ruling in favour of a plaintiff a Californian Judge cited the States' Victims' Bill of Right and stated, 'Safe, secure and peaceful schools are constitutionally mandatory'.

But it is to the Scandinavian countries that we have to look for long-term concern about the problem. Their research tradition goes back two decades, to when the term 'mobbing' was used to describe a group attack on a deviant individual. In 1988 the Norwegians concluded a five year government funded National Campaign Against Bullying which, in addition to producing the most comprehensive quantitative data, has also supplied schools with materials to involve teachers, parents and pupils in an anti-bullying programme. (More will be written about the Norwegians' pioneer work in subsequent pages.) Their national campaign began in 1983 following the suicides of two teenagers, which were attributed to long-standing victimization (Roland, 1988).

In the United Kingdom we too have experienced the dramatic consequences of bullying; none more tragic than the events at Burnage High School in 1986 which resulted in the murder in the playground of Ahmed Ullah, a 13 year old Asian boy, by Darren Coulburn, who had a history of disruptive and bullying behaviour. An Inquiry into the events leading up to the murder was headed by Ian Macdonald QC, a senior barrister in London. A full report of the Inquiry's findings was refused publication by both local and national government and so the panel produced their own report 'Murder in the Playground' (Macdonald et al., 1989). In their conclusions the panel note:

> Although we are clear that the murder was racist as we defined it, it was also a much more complexed event and raised other equally important issues. . . . There is nothing in the evidence to suggest that a murder of this kind could have taken place at Burnage High School. It could have happened in any number of other schools in Manchester or the United Kingdom. (Macdonald et al., 1989)

In the last four years there has been a range of initiatives in the

UK, one of the more significant being the Gulbenkian Foundation's involvement. They have funded a number of projects, including the publication of 'Bullying: A Positive Response' (Tattum and Herbert, 1990) and the setting up of Bullying Line, a specialist helpline within ChildLine. This facility ran for three months, 1st March to 31st May 1990, and has now been included in the wider counselling of ChildLine. During that short time Bullying Line answered more than 7,600 calls and counsellors wrote up notes on 2,054 calls (Fontaine and Lazarus, 1991). These figures are a further indication of the extent of the problem. Another valuable project was the production of an annotated bibliography on bullying (Skinner, 1991).

In 1990 the Foundation also sponsored a Survey Service for schools, based at Sheffield University, Department of Psychology. The survey results in a portfolio which will give the receiving school a great deal of information on the extent and nature of bully/victim problems in that school. Most encouragingly, the DES has acknowledged the seriousness of bullying and funded the extension of the above pilot study. This action programme aims to develop a range of intervention strategies for schools. The project director in both instances is Dr Peter K. Smith.

WHAT IS BULLYING?

Bullying is a complex problem and it may be that one of the reasons why we have failed to give it greater attention is that we hold too simplistic a view and subscribe to the idea that it is a transient experience with only short-term consequences. In Tattum and Lane (1989) and Tattum and Herbert (1990) the following six elements of bullying are discussed: nature, intensity, duration, intentionality, numbers involved and motivation. Bullying can be physical and/or verbal in nature. Physical assault to varying degrees of severity is distressing but the main weapons of the bully are threat and fear. Name-calling, teasing and verbal abuse are just as emotionally bruising, and other psychologically damaging behaviour would include intimidation, extortion, exclusion and the spreading of malicious rumours.

Particularly disturbing forms of bullying are sexual and racial abuse. The former demeans girls and women, and the latter is an attack on an individual's family, culture and community. Unfortunately, some teachers give tacit support to the above forms of abuse by the way they address children and young people. Consider the following example from the Commission for Racial Equality's Report (1988):

At a primary school in the North-West a black child was forced by the teacher to stand up and spell out the word 'golliwog' when the child refused to read it out in class because he found it offensive.

Another vulnerable group are disabled pupils. Consider the case of Rebecca who has suffered from cerebral palsy since her birth. Her speech is slow and her movement laboured but her intelligence and determination are exceptional. In the summer of 1990 she took her GCSEs, in nine subjects, and got A grades in them all. Becky was also a member of the school's popular steel band but a group of teenage girls made her life a misery because they thought that she did not fit in with the image they thought the band should portray; Becky and her sister were forced to leave the band. (Observer, 28th April 1991)

There are a number of definitions of bullying and the following by Roland (1988) is comprehensive.

Bullying is long-standing violence, physical or psychological, conducted by an individual or a group and directed against an individual who is not able to defend himself in the actual situation.

In addition, we offer another very short definition because it enables us to emphasize two particular factors in bully-victim interaction.

Bullying is a wilful, conscious desire to hurt another and put him/her under stress. (Tattum, 1989)

The authors hold the view that bullies know what they are doing and that it is wrong. Intentionality is in the first instance linked to age, and Maccoby (1980) emphasized the need for a child to reach an appropriate level of cognitive development, that is, an understanding of self and the feelings of others. Patterson *et al.* (1967) gives examples of aggression in 3- to 4-year-old nursery school children, maintaining that even at this early age some children were learning that aggressive acts could have a successful and rewarding outcome. Manning *et al.* (1978) in her research with 3- to 5-year-olds makes the distinction between 'harassment', that is, unprovoked aggression which a child found rewarding, and 'game hostility', which is very rough and intimidatory behaviour in the course of a fantasy game. From the other child's position fantasy play spills over into bullying when the aggressor's behaviour causes him/her to be afraid.

The above definition also emphasizes the stress under which a victim may be placed. The bully does not have to be physically present for a child to become apprehensive and anxious about travelling to school or using the toilets. In fact, Reid (1988) 'found that bullying was the initial reason given by 15 per cent of a sample of persistent absentees for first missing school. The same group indicated that it is one of the major reasons for their continued absence from school in 19 per cent of cases'.

Frequency is also a factor to be considered and we do not regard isolated incidents, however severe, as bullying. In cases we have encountered the victims have suffered for weeks, months or years. Bullying gangs can terrorize a playground and it is probably the case that gang bullying can be more unpleasant and harmful to the victim. Stephenson and Smith (1988) found that 41 per cent of bullies said they encouraged other children to join with them in bullying. The message is that where there is a bullying gang no one is safe. In Tattum and Herbert (1990) a distinction is made between children who are 'supporters' or 'spectators' and at this level teachers need to challenge children in their classes to consider their position – for if they are not part of the solution then they are part of the problem.

In their bullying, boys are more likely to inflict physical assaults while girls tend to use more psychological methods, such as name-calling and exclusion from the group. Bullies are overly aggressive and destructive, and they enjoy dominating other children so that they quickly misinterpret an innocent bump or careless intrusion as an attack or insult. In other words, their victims may be any unfortunate who crosses their path, so that the traditional stereotype of a victim as someone who is overtly different in their appearance or behaviour over-simplifies the complex nature of bully–victim interaction.

The traditional view that wearing glasses, having red hair, fatness and so on, can cause a child to be a victim does not necessarily apply. In fact, they are often *post facto* adult rationalizations. Generally speaking, however, victims tend to be physically weaker than other children whilst bullies are stronger and bigger than average (Olweus, 1984). In an attempt to extend our understanding of the problem Stephenson and Smith (1988) distinguish between bullies and anxious bullies, and victims and provocative victims. Furthermore, it is incorrect to assume that children are either one or the other, for some bullies are also victims.

THE INCIDENCE OF BULLYING

The most reliable data on how much bullying there is in schools come from the Scandinavian countries. A national survey of 140,000 Norwegian junior and senior high school students calculated that 6 per cent of the population are bullies and 9 per cent are harassed and attacked by them. If we were to apply these figures to Britain, with a school population of 9.6 million children in state schools, then the staggering figure of about 1.3 million are or will be involved in bully–victim problems; and as there are 35,000 state schools it means that no school can claim exemption –

it happens in all schools. Admittedly, it is never satisfactory to transpose data from one country to another because of cultural, social, demographic and educational differences. The regional research in Britain, however, does support these dramatic figures but there is certainly need for research on a national scale to ascertain the true extent of the problem. Confirmatory data can be found in the Newson and Newson (1984) longitudinal study where they reported that out of a sample of 700 11-year-olds, the mothers of 26 per cent were aware that their children were being bullied at school, 4 per cent seriously, and another 22 per cent were being bullied in the street. Stephenson and Smith (1988) also present high regional figures using self-report and teacher ratings. They found a high measure of agreement between the two groups and a figure of 23 per cent of their 1,078 sample of final year primary school pupils were identified as being involved as either victims or bullies.

In Scotland Mellor (1990), who used a similar definition and questionnaire to the Norwegian survey, produced similar figures to Norway, namely, 9 per cent victims and 6 per cent bullies. On the other hand, a number of other studies, using virtually the same instruments, provide even more disturbing figures. From a study of 2,000 pupils in middle/secondary schools in South Yorkshire Ahmad and Smith (1989) found that one in five had been bullied and one in ten had bullied others. Similar findings for secondary schools were reported by Yates and Smith (1989), in a study which involved 234 pupils in two secondary schools, also in the South Yorkshire area.

THE LONG-TERM EFFECTS OF BULLYING

Evidence strongly suggests that bullying tends to be an inter-generational problem. In a 22-year longitudinal study carried out in the USA, Eron and his associates (1987) found that young bullies have about a one in four chance of having a criminal record by age 30, whilst other children have a one in twenty chance of becoming adult criminals. The researchers studied 870 children from age 8 to age 30. Of the 427 children traced at age 19, those who had been most aggressive as young children were more likely to have dropped out of school and have delinquent records. Of the 409 who were traced at age 30 most tended to have children who were bullies, to abuse their wives and children, and to have more convictions for violent crimes.

In Norway, Olweus (1989) also writes of bullying as a 'component of a more generally anti-social and rule-breaking behaviour pattern'. From his follow-up studies he found that:

Approximately 60 per cent of boys who were characterized as

bullies in grades 6–9 had at least one court conviction at the age of 24. Even more dramatically, as much as 35–40 per cent of the former bullies had three or more court convictions at this age while this was true of only 10 per cent of the control boys (those who were neither bullies nor victims in grades 6–9). Thus, as young adults the former bullies had a fourfold increase in the level of relatively serious, recidivist criminality. (Olweus, 1989)

It is evident that bullying is a serious problem which we can no longer ignore or dismiss with adult cliches. It is a pattern of destructive behaviour which, if not changed, will have disastrous consequences for subsequent generations of children and society at large. Aggressive behaviour is learned. Living with parents who abuse them teaches children that aggression and violence are effective and acceptable means to dominate others and get your own way. For the victim the long-term consequences are also distressing, especially if it is experienced persistently over a long period. They often feel isolated by their experience and wonder what is wrong with them that they should be singled out. They may even begin to feel that they deserve the taunts, teasing and harassment and become withdrawn and less willing to take social, intellectual or vocational risks. In extreme cases they take these feelings of inadequacy into adult life. Their feelings of self-reproach are part of the reason why they are reluctant to confide in their parents or teachers.

ADULT ATTITUDES TO BULLYING

It is difficult to understand why the education community in general has been so 'blinkered'. For all who have attended schools as pupils and teachers know that bullying is persistent and widespread. Can it be that pupil victimization is regarded as an inevitable part of school life, with its initiation ceremonies, rough and tumble of boisterous play or friendly teasing? Adults are also prone to dismiss it with hollow cliches, such as 'boys will be boys', 'it's part of growing up', 'they'll grow out of it'. Yet how many adults would tolerate abuse and harassment in their workplace without turning for support from a recognized person or organization?

Another thought on adult attitudes to bullying is contained in the rhyme: 'tell tale tit, your tongue should be slit'. Only thoughtless adults could burden a child with such a fearful rule, for such an injunction is a 'bully's charter'. The bully is protected by a misplaced code of secrecy amongst children but this rhyme reinforces it by suggesting that a worse offence is to be a tell-tale, a sneak, or a grass. It is a rule which is kept by confused, vulnerable children who are told by adults to be truthful and honest and are abandoned by those same authorities when they turn to them for help.

Pupil victims are also reluctant to tell parents and teachers for fear of inciting further hostile behaviour. Victims are ashamed of what is happening to them as they think that they are the only one being singled out. This causes them to believe that there really is something wrong with them and in extreme cases assume an attitude of self-reproach and guilt. As argued earlier there is also a misplaced view that because bullying takes place when teachers are not about, they do not know who are bullies and who are victims.

Another serious concern is developed by Askew (1988) which is that, especially in boys' secondary schools and to a lesser extent in mixed secondary schools, the masculine ethos portrays, and hence encourages, aggressiveness and bullying. Boys are expected to be competitive, dominant, forceful and ambitious – an implicit code of toughness, not being afraid to fight, and being able to look after yourself is evident. Bluntly stated, some teachers are bullies and present aggressive models for pupils to learn that domination and intimidation is how to get your own way.

A WHOLE-SCHOOL APPROACH TO COUNTER BULLYING

If we are to effectively begin to cope with the problem of bullying we need to acknowledge its prevalence and understand more fully its origin and motivation. As it is a secretive activity we need strategies which approach the issues from an alternative route to the present reactive, crisis-management response, the aim of which is to change attitudes towards bullying and at the same time create a school ethos that will not tolerate the oppression of one member by another. The aim must be for a whole-school policy which is consistent with the daily experiences of teachers, pupils and parents. Individual schools must look to heighten the awareness of teaching and non-teaching staff so that they are more alert to the extent of bullying and its long-term effects on both parties. This may require a survey to convince some teachers of its prevalence and frequency in their school (Ahmad and Smith, 1990).

At the centre of its whole-school approach a school must have a policy on how it may be tackled and reduced. To this end a policy statement must be drawn up and communicated to all parents and pupils. The Governing Body should be involved in its preparation and reiteration, as the 1986 and 1988 Education Act charge them with legal responsibility for the conduct of the school and discipline. The Advisory Centre for Education has produced an invaluable information sheet on 'Governors and Bullying' (ACE, 1990).

Some of the reasons why a school needs a whole-school policy statement and elements of its approach are developed below.

A WHOLE-SCHOOL POLICY

Reasons

1. *To counter the view that bullying is an inevitable part of school life* – and so challenge teachers' and pupils' attitudes towards agressive behaviour and examine their relationships with each other, not just pupil–pupil but also teacher–teacher and teacher–pupil relationships. A school has to decide whether it 'unintentionally' reinforces or discourages aggressive behaviour.

2. *To move beyond a crisis-management approach* which only reacts to critical cases and permits some headteachers to deny that bullying happens in their school. The 'elements' discussed later will enable a school to progress into a more preventative ethos.

3. *To open up discussion at all levels* from a full staff development day to class/tutorial groups. In this way bullying will no longer be looked upon as a secret activity affecting the few. For it is this climate which discourages victims and those who witness bullying from speaking out and, also, encourages the bully to continue unashamed because the behaviour is not named in an overall condemnatory climate.

4. *To involve more people in the identification and condemnation of bullying.* In their 1982 survey Stephenson and Smith made a study of six primary schools with the highest and six primary schools with the lowest incidence of bullying. 'In all but one of the low bullying schools the teachers expressed articulate, considered and also purposeful views on bullying which emphasized the need for prevention whereas this was less apparent in the high bullying schools. The responses suggest that there was an agreed policy on bullying in the low bullying schools.' (Stephenson and Smith, 1988).

5. *To draw up an agreed set of procedures for staff to follow when inquiring into a case of bullying.* For it is only when documented profiles are produced that a school will be able to isolate bullying individuals and break up bullying gangs. It is also better if procedures are drawn up, since it is much easier to deal with confrontations about discipline in a calm atmosphere before there is a difficult incident, if there are agreed ground rules.

6. *To create a supportive climate and break down the code of secrecy.* When bullying is reported by pupils or parents it must be taken seriously and acted upon in a way which discourages the bully without humiliating the victim. Children are reluctant

to tell because they fear the consequences, not only from the bully but also from adults. Some are reluctant to believe or dismiss the victim's allegations with counter accusations of provocation or their parents as being over-protective. All of which is tantamount to blaming the victim for the bully's aggression.

7. *To provide a safe, secure learning environment for all pupils* – for this is the right of every child and young person attending our schools and colleges. Pupils cannot satisfactorily do their work if they are burdened with anxiety, humiliation and fear.

Elements

1. *A Policy statement declaring the unacceptability of bullying.* This statement should be collectively drawn up by staff (widely conceived) and governors so that all adults directly associated with the school feel that they have been involved in the school's anti-bullying declaration, which will result in their greater commitment. The statement should begin by positively expressing the school's standards and expectations, and then proceed to naming those behaviours which will not be tolerated and the consequences for anyone who persistently breaches the statement.

   Research demonstrates that aggression in children can manifest itself in different ways and towards different targets. In school it could mean bullying, disruption, vandalism and theft. Therefore, a school which sets out to counter bullying will also have a positive effect on reducing other forms of anti-social behaviour (Olweus, 1989). Another positive outcome reported by Olweus is that truancy is reduced because children are no longer afraid to attend school and actually express greater satisfaction with school life.

   A very interesting parallel research project is being directed by Roland; it is called the Janus Project. In addition to an investigation into the Campaign against Bullying the study is examining leadership in the classroom, social structures in the class and different behaviour problems, such as bullying, use of stimulants, disruption, truancy and school phobia, theft and delinquency (Roland, 1988; 1989).

2. *A multi-level approach involving a wide range of people.* It is important that teaching and non-teaching staff are involved in the discussions and implementation of an anti-bullying programme. Most bullying takes place around the school grounds – in the playground, toilets, dinner queues and in a variety of other locations. It takes place during school hours at times when pupils are less closely supervised. Therefore, to counter the secretive element of bullying every school

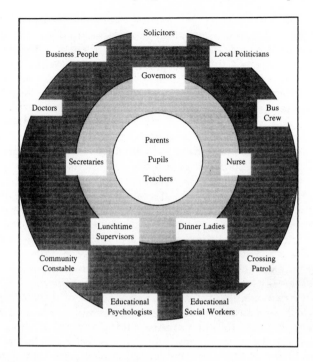

Figure 4.1 Spheres of involvement

should use the large number of employees who are not teachers.

The model 'Spheres of Involvement' (Tattum and Herbert, 1992) illustrates the wide range of people who can work with the school as part of its whole-school (even community) approach to bullying. Specific advice for parents can be found in Tattum and Herbert (1990) and Item 4 below lists a set of procedures for teachers. Prefects (or senior pupils) are particular members of the student body who can be used to discourage bullying. They should be talked to about their own attitudes and behaviour as they use or misuse their authority or position in the school.

Secretaries, nurse, dinner ladies and lunchtime supervisors can be positively used to discourage bullying. The nurse gathers all kinds of information as she dresses cuts and calms upset tummies, not least the underlying cause of the wound or the source of distress. Lunchtime supervisors operate in the heat of the playground action where it is often difficult to distinguish between real fear and pretend in fantasy games or fighting. Schools often expect too much of untrained supervisors, and there is a strong case for developing some in-house training for them.

The outside circle represents a very wide range of people who, at different times, may be involved in cases of bullying. Bus crews and Crossing Persons can help a school identify bullies and bullying gangs as they have close witness of pupil behaviour to and from school. The police, doctors and solicitors are increasingly being brought in by families to handle the more extreme cases of physical and verbal bullying. Educational psychologists meet with individual cases but more and more look to have a positive and active role in working with a school on its anti-bullying programme. Finally, an important group of professionals are the Educational Social Workers or Education Welfare Officers who meet the problem at the interface between the home and the school. Of all the forms of anti-social behaviour bullying is the one which can bring parents and teachers most into confrontation about the interpretation and response to the problem.

3. *There is a need for both long-term and short-term strategies.* In the previous section examples were given of the successes achieved as a result of the Norwegian nationwide intervention campaign. The main components of this campaign, which was aimed at teachers, parents and pupils, were a 32-page booklet for all parents, and a survey of schools. In Bergen there was a 50 per cent decrease in bully/victim problems during the two years following the campaign, for both boys and girls (Olweus, 1989). Roland (1988), although more cautious in his analysis of data gathered in Stavanger, supports the finding that there was a reduction in bullying problems in schools which displayed a commitment to the use of the materials and programme in general.

Unfortunately, we do not have a nationwide intervention programme in the United Kingdom but the materials presented in this section on a whole-school policy provide the basis for individual schools to develop their own intervention programme. To support them there is a growing supply of resource materials, and strongly recommended are Tattum and Lane (1988), Tattum and Herbert (1990) and Besag (1989). Together they provide lists of children's literature, role play and simulation exercises, videos and useful addresses to contact.

Tattum and Herbert (1991) have also produced a series of videos for staff development days, which tackle bullying in three different ways – administrative and organizational procedures, the curriculum and the school and the wider community. Examples of 'good practice' are also available in a report demonstrating the different ways in which primary and secondary schools have set up anti-bullying programmes (Tattum and Herbert, 1992).

4. *A wide discussion of bullying to open up the issues and tackle what is a*

complex problem. The reasons for wider discussion have already been rehearsed but in order to counter bullying there needs to be a detailed set of guidelines for teachers. The following list is from *Bullying: A Positive Response* (Tattum and Herbert, 1990).

ADVICE AND GUIDANCE
FOR TEACHERS

Watch for early signs of distress in pupils – deterioration of work, spurious illness, isolation, the desire to remain with adults, erractic attendance. Whilst this behaviour may be symptomatic of other problems, it may be the early signs of bullying.

Listen carefully and record all incidents.

Offer the victim immediate support and help by putting the school's procedures into operation.

Make the unacceptable nature of the behaviour, and the consequences of any repetition, clear to the bully and his/her parents.

Ensure that all accessible areas of the school are patrolled at break, lunchtime, between lessons and at the end of the day.

Use all the pupils as a positive resource in countering bullying. Peer counselling groups may be used to resolve problems. Pupils can also be used to help shy children or newcomers feel welcome and accepted. Sexual and racial harassment also need to be discussed and dealt with.

The following steps may be followed in recording incidents of bullying and also as a means of conveying to all concerned how seriously the school regards bullying behaviour.

The bullied pupil should record the events *in writing.*

The bully should also record the events *in writing.*

The teacher and/or a senior colleague should record their discussions with both parties.

The parents/carers of the pupils involved should be sent copies of all reports, and the reports placed in the respective pupils' files for a *specified* period of time.

The parents/carers of the pupils should be asked to respond to the above *in writing.*

(Tattum and Herbert, 1990)

---

82   Learning to Behave

5. *An anti-bullying campaign needs to be integrated within the school curriculum.* If we are to tackle bullying behaviour at a school-wide level then it is not sufficient to only focus on one-off periods in a pastoral or PSE programme. Neither can it be left to occasional exhortations in morning assembly. The curriculum, both formal and informal, is a vehicle for influencing pupils' perceptions, attitudes and values. There-fore, we must use it in a planned way within a whole-school response to the problem of bullying.

A curriculum approach could be tackled through a single subject or developed as part of a cross-curricular programme (Herbert, 1988). If one were to adopt a single subject, for example English, then the approach could be initiated through the reading of an appropriate children's book – Tattum and Herbert (1990) provide extensive lists appropri-ate for both primary and secondary aged pupils. For the primary school, *The Diddakoi* by Rumer Godden, provides abundant opportunities to discuss bullying through what happens to a young girl, Kizzy, who is half gypsy. In the secondary school one could use *The Chocolate War* and its sequel *Beyond the Chocolate War*, by Robert Cormier, which describe how a bully and his gang dominate and corrupt a school.

From this starting point a curriculum development plan could extend the word into Maths, in the form of a school survey, and Design Technology, by identifying bullying 'no-go' places in the school and its surrounding play areas. The work could be extended into Drama, Art, History, RE and PE, in fact, the range is only limited by the National Curriculum. In the videos and workpacks developed by Tattum and Herbert (1991) a curriculum approach is presented along the lines described in this section.

Of the cross-curricular themes identified by the National Curriculum Council the document on Education for Citizen-ship (NCC, 1990) provides an excellent format of ideas to deal with knowledge, skills, attitudes and values – and much of the content could easily be used to focus on bullying.

REFERENCES

ACE Bulletin 34 (1990) Governors and Bullying, London: ACE.
Ahmad, Y and Smith, P K (1989) *Bully/victim problems among schoolchildren*, Poster presented at conference of the Developmental Section of the BPS, Guildford.
Ahmad, Y and Smith, P K (1990) Behavioural measures: bullying in schools, *Newsletter of Association for Child Psychology and Psychiatry*, July.
Askew, S (1988) Aggressive Behaviour in Boys: to what extent is it

institutionalized? in Tattum D and Lane D (eds) *Bullying in Schools*, Stoke-on-Trent: Trentham Books.

Besag, V E (1989) *Bullies and Victims in Schools*, Milton Keynes: Open University Press.

Commission for Racial Equality (1988) *Learning in Terror!* A survey of racial harassment in schools and colleges, London: CRE.

DES (1989) Elton Report: *Discipline in Schools*, London: HMSO.

Eron, L D, Huesmann, L R, Dubow, E, Romanoff, R and Yarmel, P W (1987) Aggression and its correlates over 22 years, in Crowell, D, Evans I and O'Donnell C. (eds) *Childhood Agression and Violence*, New York: Plenum Press.

Fontaine, J La and Lazarus, G (1991) *Report on the Bullying Line*, London: Childline.

Herbert, G (1988) A Whole-Curriculum Approach to Bullying, in Tattum D and Lane D (eds) *Bullying in Schools*, Stoke-onTrent: Trentham Books.

Maccoby, E E (1980) *Social Development: Psychological growth and parent-child relationship*, New York: Harcourt Brace Jovanovich.

Macdonald, I, Bhavnani, R, Kahn, L and John, G (1989). *Murder in the Playground. The Report of the Macdonald Inquiry into racism and racial violence in Manchester schools*, London: Longsight Press.

Manning, M, Heron, J and Marshall, T (1978) Styles of hostility and social interactions at nursery, at school and at home, in Hersor, L and Berger, M (eds) *Aggression and Anti-Social Behaviour in Childhood and Adolescence*, Oxford: Pergamon Press.

Mellor, A (1990) Bullying in Scottish secondary schools, *Spotlights* 23, Edinburgh: SCRE.

National Curriculum Council (1990) *Curricular Guidance 8: Education for Citizenship*, York: NCC.

Newson, J and Newson, E (1984) Parents' Perspectives on Children's Behaviour in School, in Frude N and Gault G (eds) *Disruptive Behaviour in Schools*, Chichester: Wiley.

The Observer (1991) One girl's fight to beat the bullies in the band, 28 April.

Olweus, D (1978) *Aggression in the schools: Bullies and whipping boys*, Washington DC: Hemisphere.

Olweus, D (1984) Agressors and their victims: bullying in schools, in Frude N and Gault G (eds) *Disruptive Behaviour in Schools*, Chichester: Wiley.

Olweus, D (1989) Bully/victim problems among schoolchildren: basic facts and effects of a school based intervention programme, in Rubin K and Pepler D (eds) *The development and treatment of childhood aggression*, Hillsdale, NJ: Erlbaum.

Patterson, G R, Littman, R A and Bricker, W (1967) Assertive behaviour in young children: a step towards a theory of aggression, *Monographs of the Society for Research in Child Development*, **35**, 5.

Reid, K (1988) Bullying and Persistent School Absenteeism, in Tattum D and Lane D (eds) *Bullying in Schools*, Stoke-on-Trent: Trentham Books.

Roland, E (1988) Bullying: The Scandinavian Research Tradition, in Tattum D and Lane D (eds) *Bullying in Schools*, Stoke-on-Trent: Trentham Books.

Roland, E (1989) A system oriented strategy against bullying, in Roland E and Munthe E (eds) *Bullying: An International Perspective*, London: David Fulton Pub.

Skinner, A (1991) *Annotated Bibliography on Bullying*, Leicestei: National Youth Agency.

Smith, P K (1991) The Silent Nightmare: Bullying and Victimisation in School Peer Groups, *The Psychologist*.

Stephenson, P and Smith D (1988) Bullying in the Junior School, in Tattum D and Lane D (eds) *Bullying in Schools*, Stoke-on-Trent, Trentham Books.

Tattum, D P (1989) Bullying – a problem crying out for attention, *Pastoral Care in Education*, 7, 2, 21–5.

Tattum, D P and Herbert, G (1990) *Bullying: A Positive Response, Advice for Parents, Governors and Staff in Schools*, Cardiff: Cardiff Institute of Higher Education.

Tattum, D P and Herbert, G (1991) *Bullying: a whole-school approach*, Videos and Workpack, Cardiff: Drake Educational.

Tattum D P and Herbert, G (1992) *Countering Bullying: A Report on Good Practice in Schools and Local Authorities*, Cardiff: Cardiff Institute of Higher Education.

Tattum, D P and Lane, D (1989) *Bullying in Schools*, Stoke-on-Trent: Trentham Books.

Yates, ⁏ and Smith, P K (1989) Bullying in two English comprehensive schools, in Roland E and Munthe E (eds) *Bullying: An International Perspective*, London: David Fulton Pub.

Chapter 5

Bullying: Pupil Relationships

Helen Cowie, Michael J. Boulton and Peter K. Smith

INTRODUCTION

Bullying appears to be quite pervasive in schools, and probably to a greater extent than most teachers and parents realize, since many victims keep quiet about it. After decades of virtual neglect, three books on the topic appeared in 1989: D Tattum and D Lane (eds), *Bullying in Schools*; E Roland and E Munthe (eds), *Bullying: An International Perspective*; and V Besag, *Bullies and Victims in Schools*. From 1989 dates also a marked upsurge of public interest in the topic, accompanied by at times intensive media publicity. Coinciding with this increased public awareness is a greater knowledge both of the nature of the problem, and of what can be done about it.

The Elton Report (DES, 1989) on discipline in schools, although primarily on teacher–pupil relations and discipline, does mention problems of bullying in a few paragraphs. It states that:

> Recent studies of bullying in schools suggest that the problem is widespread and tends to be ignored by teachers. . . . Research suggests that bullying not only causes considerable suffering to individual pupils but also has a damaging effect on school atmosphere . . . .
> We therefore recommend that headteachers and staff should: be alert to signs of bullying and racial harassment; deal firmly with all such behaviour; and take action based on clear rules which are backed by appropriate sanctions and systems to protect and support victims.
> (op. cit., pp. 102–3).

The extent of bully/victim problems

Researchers working in various countries have shown that bullying problems are extensive during middle childhood and early adolescence. Most of this work has been carried out within schools, probably because it is in this environment of high densities of young people that bullying is particularly likely to occur. Olweus (1978, 1989) devised a self-report questionnaire which was administered to over 140,000 Norwegian students aged between 8 and 16 years. About 9 per cent reported being bullied, and about 7 per cent reported bullying others, 'now and then' or more frequently. Other researchers working outside of Scandinavia have since employed versions of Olweus' questionnaire with equally or even more disturbing results (Smith, 1991). The lowest figures are from Scotland, where Mellor (1990) found 6 per cent of reported victims and 4 per cent of bullies in a sample of secondary school children. But in Ireland, O'Moore and Hillery (1989) found that out of nearly 800 Dublin school children aged 7–13 years old about 10 per cent reported being involved in 'serious' bullying (once a week or more frequently), either as aggressors or as victims. A survey we have recently completed of some 7,000 pupils in 24 junior, middle and secondary schools in South Yorkshire shows that while there are variations between schools, the figures just quoted are not unrepresentative (Whitney and Smith, 1991). In junior/middle schools an average of 27 per cent of pupils reported being bullied 'sometimes' or more, and 10 per cent 'once a week' or more; for secondary schools the average figures were 10 per cent and 4 per cent respectively.

Our confidence in the anonymous questionnaire used in these surveys is enhanced by the general consistency children show in answering the 25 or so separate questions. Most pupils treat the exercise very seriously. The questionnaires can be used to provide a school with a detailed survey of the nature and extent of bully/victim problems in different classes and year groups (Ahmad, Whitney and Smith, 1991).

As an alternative to a questionnaire approach, we have also asked children to nominate those classmates who were bullies and those who were victims, having ensured that they understand these terms. This gives a slightly different metric and perspective on the problem. Each child receives nominations as 'bully' or 'victim' from between 0 per cent and 100 per cent of classmates; we can then take a cutoff of, say, 33 per cent or 50 per cent nominations to designate children of particular concern as a bully or victim. This method was used to identify children, some of whom are discussed further in the middle section of this chapter.

The nature of bullying

Whatever method of assessment we use, it is clear that bully-victim problems are widespread. The questionnaire surveys have also given us considerable information on the nature of bully/victim problems (Whitney and Smith, 1991). Most of the children or young people who report being bullied say that it takes the form of teasing; but about a third report other forms such as hitting or kicking, or (more occasionally) extortion of money. These latter may seem the more serious forms, but some 'teasing', especially that related to some disability, or which takes the form of racial or sexual harassment, can be very hurtful.

A common finding is that boys are more likely than girls to be doing the bullying, whereas the two sexes are about equally likely to be on the receiving end. Also, most boys report being bullied by male peers only, while girls generally indicate tht they were picked on by children of either sex. The actual forms of bullying experienced by the two sexes differ to some extent. Girls are more likely to resort to verbal and 'psychological' types of bullying, such as excluding an individual from their activities and spreading unpleasant rumours, whereas boys more often use physically aggressive acts. However, these findings are of general trends; we have come across cases of girls resorting to physical bullying, as well as of boys using subtle psychological tactics.

Most of the bullying reported is by children or young people in the same class or at least the same year as the victim. Some is by older pupils, but not surprisingly little is by younger pupils.

Victims are more likely to report being alone at break time (for example, Farana and Graham in the case studies later), and to feel less well liked at school; having some good friends can be a strong protective factor against being bullied. However, this potential support needs to be harnessed; most pupils did not think that peers would be very likely to help stop a child being bullied.

By contrast, many pupils thought that a teacher would try to stop bullying. Despite this general perception, only a minority of victims report that they have talked to a teacher or anyone at home about it, or that a teacher or parent has talked to them about it. Teachers are often not aware of bullying in the playground, since supervision at break time is now undertaken by lunchtime supervisory assistants (who usually receive little if any training for the job). Not all approaches to teachers are sympathetically received, and unless the school has a very definite and effective policy, the bullied child may well feel afraid of retribution for 'telling'. Victims are also often unwilling to involve their parents, partly because they may blame themselves, partly because of embarrassment and possible unforeseen consequences if the parents go to complain to the school.

Consequences of being bullied, or of bullying others

Relatively few researchers have examined the stability of a child's propensity to bully peers or be bullied by them, but the available evidence suggests at least a fair degree of stability in both cases. In Norway, Olweus (1978) found that many children who were classified as bullies and victims at 13 years could be similarly classified some three years later, even despite a change in classes, teachers and/or schools. In a study involving 8- and 9-year-olds (Boulton and Smith, 1991), we examined stability in these areas across four assessment periods that were roughly equally spaced between the beginning of one school year and the start of the next. For children identified either as bullies, or as victims, by a third or more of their peers, there was evidence for a high degree of stability.

How much does this behaviour matter? For children being bullied, their lives are being made miserable often for some considerable period of time. Already probably lacking close friends at school, they are likely to lose confidence and self-esteem even further. The peer rejection which victims often experience is a strong predictor of later adult disturbance (Parker and Asher, 1987). Research by Gilmartin (1987), using retrospective data, found that some 80 per cent of 'love-shy' men (who despite being heterosexual found it very difficult to have relationships with the opposite sex) had experienced bullying or harassment at school. The most severe consequences of bullying can be the actual suicide of the victim, or their death as a direct or indirect result of bullying, as in the Burnage High School case (Burnage Report, 1989).

There are also consequences for those who bully others. They are learning that power-assertive and sometimes violent behaviour can be used to get their own way (see the case study of Mark, later). Unless counteracted, such forms of behaviour can continue and lead to further undesirable outcomes. A follow-up by Olweus (1989) in Norway, of secondary school pupils to age 24, found that former school bullies were nearly four times more likely than non-bullies to have had three or more court convictions. In the UK, Lane (1989) found involvement in bullying at school to be a strong predictor of delinquency. There is other evidence generally suggesting poor long-term outcomes for children with 'deviant' type behaviour conduct disorders (Robins, 1986; Rutter, 1989).

CASE STUDY REPORTS
(NB: all the children's names are pseudonyms)

The following ethnographic accounts, gathered from children involved in bullying or being bullied, their peers, and teachers, were gathered from a middle school in a disadvantaged area of Sheffield. The school is taking part in a co-operative group work intervention project, funded by the Education and Science Research Council (Smith, Boulton and Cowie, 1989).

Farana and Graham: victims of bullying

Farana and Graham are both very quiet children and easily overlooked in class. When the teacher asks children to take partners for an activity, they are seldom chosen; at break time they are likely to be alone.

Farana was nominated as a victim by 42 per cent of the children in her class. She considers herself to be lucky that there is one girl who will occasionally play with her, but for much of the time her experience of peer relationships is a negative one:

> Some people hurt me in my class. They swear, sort of. They call me names. ... Sometimes they don't like me because I'm Pakistani. They don't like me. They think I'm *just* a Pakistani.

At break time Farana can never be sure that she will have a playmate:

> HC: some children get ignored by other children in the school and often feel lonely. Do you ever feel lonely like this?
> Farana: Yes, when I've no friends – when Joanne's not my friend, when my sisters are inside at school.
> HC: Have you tried to be friendly with them?
> Farana (quietly): Sometimes. They won't be my friends.

In fact, if Farana tries to join in group games, it is a common experience for her to find that someone will actively force her out:

> HC: Is there anyone you don't get on with very well?
> Farana: Yes, Chris. He don't let me take part.
> HC: What does he do to keep you out?
> Farana: He does nearly everything. He calls me names.

Sadly when Farana walks around on her own in the playground she can be the target of further bullying. Her teacher, Mr W., points out: 'She is vulnerable in the playground. Children like Darren will kick Farana. He can pick his people well! He picks people who aren't likely to hit back'. Farana is a shy child and this in itself could make it difficult for her to relate easily to her peers, but with her sisters and in some supportive small groups in class she is accepted by others and can make effective contributions to group tasks. Because of the prejudiced attitudes of some of her peers, a major reason for her victimization seems to be that she is of Asian origin.

Graham was nominated as a victim by 50 per cent of his classmates. His experience of peer relationships is similar in many ways to that of Farana, but the reasons which underlie his role as victim seem to have more to do with his introverted personality and his lack of opportunity to develop appropriate social skills. His perception of children in his class is that 'they are always fighting'. He can name two other children who will sometimes play with him. He likes them because they let him play football, but adds: 'Probably they are the only two people [in the class] who want to play with me'. Graham is not a popular choice when it comes to taking a partner because he is so shy and unforthcoming. Other children do not find him fun to be with.

As Ms H., his teacher says: 'He's very withdrawn. He doesn't give much to other children unless he is in a good mood . . . . He is just a very introverted, withdrawn person'. Graham is vulnerable to attack in the playground simply because he is often on his own. He is also excluded from many activities, especially the prestigious football games which play such an important part in the lives of boys in his age group. Probably the most alarming aspect of Graham's experience of peer relationships is that, although he is perceived as a victim by classmates, he does not consider that he has been bullied. Difficult as he finds it to talk about his loneliness and lack of contact with friends, the overriding impression is that Graham blames himself for his isolation.

Mark: a bully

Mark was nominated as a bully by 65 per cent of his classmates. He is 9 years old, tall for his age and physically fit. One of his hobbies is practising karate. He tends to see the world as a threatening place, and it is important for him to be ready to defend himself. In his words:

> Karate is defence, so if someone came up and hit you, I've got licence even to kill. You know, if you killed someone doing karate, yeah, you can't get done because it (the licence) tells you that you're doing it for self-defence.

Mark has been bullying other children since he was in first school. Here he recalls an incident from the past:

> Mark: When it was my ball, I brought it to school, he goes, 'I'll pop it' and I said, 'Will ya?' and 'I'll pop *your* brain!'. Then he popped it and I gave him one . . . [pauses] . . . he had a broken nose. I broke his nose!
>
> HC: You broke his nose?
>
> Mark: He was on the floor before it got broken. I just stamped on it like that.
>
> HC: You stamped on his nose? Were you sorry afterwards?
>
> Mark: No. . . . He admitted that he started the fight.
>
> HC: That's quite a reaction on your part now, wasn't it? To break his nose you must have stamped on it pretty hard.
>
> Mark (coolly): Not pretty hard 'cos on the side it's soft there.
>
> HC: How do you think that he felt?
>
> Mark: Nowt. He just ran out and went home.

This pattern of responding to other children with a strong counter-attack has persisted. He shows no remorse for his over-reaction since he feels fully justified and is always convinced that the victim deserved all he got.

Sometimes the only provocation on the part of the victim is that he or she is better at something. Shoukat is a boy nominated by 75 per cent of his classmates as a victim. He has had to learn that he must never allow any comparison between his school work and that of Mark or Yussef, Mark's companion. If he does, the punishment will be swift:

> Shoukat: When I'm doing good work, Mark and Yussef start confusing me. Like calling me nasty names and pushing my chair. Or they get a piece of paper and tear it and tell Miss I did it. That's what they did today. I think why they're doing it is just that they are jealous. Like they got hold of my chair and started pushing it. I said, 'Stop it!' but they wouldn't so I moved my chair to the other side of the table so they couldn't push it, and then Miss moved them, because they were messing about.

Shoukat has tried shouting back at them but without success. His strategy for survival, is now, understandably, to keep a very low profile when Mark and Yussef are around. It can be a real disadvantage to him if the teacher praises his good work:

> I do better things than them. They mess about and I draw. Then I get a sticker. So then they think, 'How come he's got a sticker?' and then they start picking on me. If I start shouting at them *they* think I'm making trouble. If I ignore them, then I get some good things like to do some cooking with Miss D.

Other children have tried confronting Mark with specific examples of aggressive behaviour but he does not find it easy to listen to honest feedback and reacts angrily to any hint of criticism from others. He will shout almost hysterically, 'Shut up' or 'You liar!', so small group evaluation sessions, which work well with most of the other children in the class, are not successful when Mark is a member of the group.

Mark's teacher is aware of the situation. She sees that some children tease and annoy him, but she has also noticed how quickly he goes on the defensive when faced with something that he does not like:

> He can be so silly. Someone will pull a face and he'll go up and say, 'Don't you do that again!' I think it's as if they offend him. He can be so aggressive. Then he'll take it to the extreme.

So far, it seems, no one has successfully challenged Mark. He has worked out that, although there are penalties for aggressive behaviour, on the whole they are a small price to pay: 'I just got to do lines for a few weeks and miss playtime'. Why should that bother him? After all, as he learned in his karate class, 'No pain, no gain'!

Alan: a bully/victim

Alan was nominated as a bully by 55 per cent of his classmates, and as a victim by 65 per cent. He is a small boy. He has been unhappy in his school for some time. As he says, with a deep sigh, 'I keep saying to my mum, "I want to leave this school 'cos people bully me before I bully them" but she says, "No".' His wish would be that 'all the bad people left and friendly people came back into school'.

Alan finds it hard to think of anything positive to say about his classmates and cannot name a particular friend. He talks mainly about arguments and fights which he defines as 'bullying'. In his words, 'only two people in the class *don't* bully me'. There is no one person whom he would choose as a partner for classwork or for play.

He readily admits that he too 'bullies' other children, for example Richard; but thinks that usually they start the fight:

> HC: What sort of things do you do when you are bullying Richard?
> Alan: Well, he starts it first, like, comes to my table, punches me on the back, then we have a fight and then we get done by the teacher.
> HC: Do you usually win these fights?
> Alan: Yes, 'cos he's only little. Sometimes he cries, sometimes he tells.

Other children confirm his quarrelsome attitude. A typical comment is:

> He thumps me in the back when we're working. He thumps me so I thump him back.

His teacher has noticed how difficult he finds it to co-operate with other children for any length of time:

> Alan and Donna, they're either very good together and help each other or they argue and want to almost kill each other. [HC: Why?]. Because they're both very painfully honest with each other. They say, 'You did it' or 'I didn't' or 'Why have you got . . .?' You know. They're both jealous of each other if the one has something that the other doesn't . . . I don't think they really like each other. But then they've got problems of their own. That comes out when they're together.

On the occasion when Alan is rash enough to annoy a stronger boy like Mark he gets into real trouble:

> Mark: Alan drew this love heart and he gave it to Michelle. He said I drew it so I went up to him and went right hard on his nose.

HC: You punched him on the nose!
Mark: It didn't break. . . . It only started bleeding.
HC: How do you think he felt when you made his nose bleed?
Mark: Sad.
HC: Sad. Did that worry you at all?
Mark: No. I knew what would happen when I did it.
HC: You mean, you knew you were going to punch him hard?
Mark: No, I do that automatically. When anyone gets me mad, I just swing me fist out. . . . It was Alan's fault 'cos he drew the love heart and gave it to Michelle. . . .

Alan has certainly contributed to his alienation from the rest of the class and can provoke attacks from other children. But a major difficulty for him is that he assumes that other children do not like him and does very little to try to win friends. As his teacher points out, he typically anticipates that he is not likely to be chosen in situations where children take partners:

He will stand up and say 'I don't want to be with anybody'. Whether he knew that nobody would pick him, I don't know. He had a hot temper and nobody wanted to be near him, I suppose.

Because Alan is quarrelsome, it is easy for others to blame him for any fights that occur. He is not a pleasant working partner and so, even in small group work, he does not sustain closeness with other children.

Sean: a bully

Sean was nominated as a bully by 68 per cent of his classmates; at the same time he is viewed 'controversially' in the sense that some children like him very much and others dislike him strongly. He is tall, physically fit and attractive. He is aware of his power to draw attention to himself and explains it as being due to: 'Good looks . . . personality . . . I'm clever at sport and just share things and that'. At the beginning of the first year of middle school, his teacher acknowledged his skill in relating to other people but showed some concern:

He's a very strong personality that usually acts for the good but has a very strong sense of devilment. And he has a very good general knowledge and lots of ideas . . . so he's a fun person to have around. But I think people's relations with him are tinged with fear. You've got to be friendly with him, otherwise . . . because he is quite tough.

Sean himself does not deny that there have been times when he abused his power in the class:

HC: Have you ever bullied anybody?
Sean: No, but I hit someone for doing something little to me.

. . . It was Robert. . . . He got on my nerves. Every time you tap him he says, 'Stop tickling me?' So I just hit him.

And he freely admits that envious feelings make it hard for him to get on with children like Robert who have 'always got the right answers and brag off about it.' This 'gets on my nerves' and, at times, causes Sean to 'lose my temper and beat him up, 'cos Robert's right good. He's always going on trips and all this and I'm not because I'm not that good because he's better than good'.

Sean has forged long-standing friendships with two other dominant boys in the class. They play football together at break and after school, and make sure that only good players are in their team. He justifies excluding 'crap players' on the grounds that: 'There's millions of footballs int' yard and they know they just want to annoy me 'cos they don't like me saying no to them'. The impression is that, while low-status children feel left out, favoured children become highly positive about Sean's personal qualities of loyalty, liveliness and sheer fun: 'He always plays football with me and he's always been friends for years' (Steve, another bully), and 'Sean makes me laugh' (Lottie, a popular girl). Yet there is also a side to Sean which is caring and supportive. He spends time helping Ian in class: 'He's not very good at reading but I can help him learn words and help him to work good – and we have a laugh'. His confidence and sense of fun allows him to play tricks on other people and get away with it:

I put drawing pins on their seats and wiggly worms in their desks. Yes, and it's funny. They know I'm going to do it because I tell them I'm going to, and then they start screaming and they get right mad at me.

The kind of practical joke which misfired so badly for Alan is hugely successful for Sean and indicates his skill at judging how people relate to one another:

Me and Ian write letters to each other and say, 'Will you go out with me;' from boys to girls and we have a laugh. I wrote one from Lottie to Ian and from Ian to Lottie and they both got them at the same time. And they both read them and they were both thinking 'Yes' and when they said 'Yes' I said I was only messing about. And then if they said 'No' I would say I was messing about but if she said 'Yes' Ian would say 'Thanks for going out with me'.

Sean, when asked, expresses prejudice in general towards black children but, paradoxically, plays with some Asian boys. His feelings towards them are ambivalent:

None of them like me because they think I hate their sisters and they are thinking, 'I hate him' behind my back, and they are always talking about me. They know if I catch them they've had it. [HC; What does that mean?] I'll knock them out because I don't like people talking about me.

Yet in the course of his first year of middle school Sean developed a strong friendship with Imtiaz who became a member of Sean's close-knit friendship group. Furthermore, he became close to Cecile, a popular Afro-Caribbean girl and spent a lot of time with her in class. His teacher noted the change in his attitude: 'Sean and Cecile are a very happy mixed sex pair. He has his arm round her during the day'. The change in Sean over the year extended to other children:

I don't think people are afraid of him now. I don't hear the same kind of bullying things in the playground. . . . He's got power. People who might not say, 'Yes' to somebody else will say, 'Yes' to Sean. He is a powerful person. There's no way you can ignore him. He impinges on everybody's life.

The children in Sean's class had, in the course of the year, been given many opportunities to work in co-operative groups. They were encouraged to share feelings and to evaluate one another as working partners in small groups. Unlike Mark, a bully who ruled by sheer force, Sean's power came from a strong and lively personality linked with a great energy and sense of fun. He also showed the capacity to listen to others in the class and seemed genuinely to think about what they thought of him. His prejudiced attitudes, expressed on issues of gender and race, were not so rigid that they could not be modified in the light of experience. He showed his capacity to respond to other children on the basis of their individual qualities and was able to discard some of his preconceived ideas. He seemed to understand that to some extent he bullied because he felt insecure or jealous. His popularity indicated that, in another sense, there was no need for him to bully, since he could win the admiration of others through his social skills, his personality and his prowess at sport.

Subgroups of children who are bullied or victimized

Although it is tempting to talk of 'bullies' and 'victims', the case studies confirm previous research studies which indicate that this is an over-simple typology. Olweus (1978) distinguished between 'passive' victims (children like Graham who are anxious, insecure, and fail to defend themselves) and 'provocative' victims (children like Alan who are hot-tempered, create tension, fight back). Perry, Kusel and Perry (1988) made a similar distinction between low-aggressive and high-aggressive victims. The former may be anxious and insecure, but do nothing actively to 'invite' attacks (Farana and Shoukat might be examples). The latter on the other hand may be characterized as having a 'short fuse', and seem deliberately to do things they know will irritate and tease others, often with the apparent aim of provoking a hostile response. Many children may act in this way at some time or another: for example a group of boys may disrupt a game of skipping being played by their female peers, and a group of girls may embarrass a boy in front of his friends by saying he 'fancies' one of the girls. Alan's attempt to play a trick on Mark illustrates this kind of 'provocative' behaviour on the part of a victim. For a small number of individuals, this pattern of interaction may become typical of their dealings with their peers.

Another typology was proposed by Stephenson and Smith (1989) on the basis of teacher reports. In particular they mentioned some children whom they described as bully/victims: children who are bullies with some of their peers but victims at the hands of others. Alan, in our case studies, is a bully/victim on the basis of peer nominations, and indeed this category may overlap quite closely with that of 'provocative' or 'high-aggressive' victims. This type of individual may be more common than was first thought – in our research work with middle school children we have found 'bully/victims' to be as common as either 'bullies' or 'victims' separately, when assessed by peer nominations. This may reflect the generally high level of teasing and harassment which may go on in these groups, where the children are from ethnically mixed backgrounds and somewhat disadvantaged circumstances. Thus, many children may be seen by others as being involved in both sides of bullying incidents.

Bullying and social relations with peers

Several studies have shown that bullies may enjoy at least average levels of popularity within the peer group, but that victims tend to be unpopular. In a sample of 158 middle school children (Boulton and Smith, 1991), we found that of the six sociometric status types identified by Coie, et al. (1982), rejected and neglected children received the most 'victim' nominations from peers (on average they were nominated as such by more than 25 per cent of classmates); popular children received the least (at 15 per cent).

Several interesting and potentially important findings have come out of the research on the relationship between children's popularity with peers and their participation in aggression. In particular, there is not a linear inverse relationship between these two variables, rather it appears that aggression in some circumstances is *positively* correlated with popularity. For example, aggression in response to provocations, and to aggression from peers, has been shown to be positively correlated with acceptance by peers (Coie et al., 1982; Lesser, 1959). The case study of Sean illustrates how a child can be both popular and a bully.

Children may respond in different ways to being bullied,

including withdrawing from the peer group. This withdrawal may be reflected in such measures as how often a child is alone, and how lonely they report feeling. Our survey data show that more victims than non-victims reported feeling lonely at school. However, it is still not clear whether this high degree of social isolation and loneliness characteristic of many victims of bullying represents withdrawal *per se* on their part, or whether they are willing to associate with their peers should those peers wish it. For some victims at least, the former may be more likely: we found that victims were reported by more of their peers to 'act shy' than were bullies and non-involved children. Graham is an example; he was not a rewarding companion to be with. Farana, by contrast, showed that although quiet, she was interested in forming friendships with others. In her case, small group work in class helped her form the basis for new friendships.

Typically, victims of bullying appear to have a low opinion of themselves, and to be anxious and insecure (Olweus, 1989); as do many socially withdrawn children (Rubin *et al.*, 1990). In our own studies, we found that victims generally perceived themselves as being less physically competent than did bullies and non-involved children, and that female victims perceived themselves as being less well accepted by their peers than did the other two groups. At present, it remains unclear if these and other aspects of low self-esteem exhibited by victims precede or follow a child's experiences of being bullied, but what little evidence there is suggests a two-way relationship.

Developmental pathways leading to victimization

What are the origins of victimization? Two different approaches have been made to explaining this: first, a social skills deficit approach; and secondly, an approach via attachment theory. Recently, a more complex approach in terms of developmental pathways has been put forward by Rubin *et al.* (1990).

One influential group of theorists (Dodge *et al.*, 1986) see the cause of many problems in peer relationships as lying in a lack of appropriate social skills. Following an information processing model of social interaction, they hypothesize that some children may interpret social signals incorrectly, or have only a very limited range of response options available. Victims may lack social skills of assertiveness, or of joining a group, or responding to provocation.

Another group of theorists see problems in peer relationships as lying in family circumstances and particularly in early parent–child attachment relationships; they feel that these relationships may 'set the scene' for future peer relationships. Attachment theorists suggest that a child develops 'internal working models' of relationships (Bowlby, 1988) which may be secure or insecure.

Troy and Sroufe (1987) related parent–child attachment type to bully–victim involvement in preschoolers. The theoretical argument is most thoroughly worked out by Renken, *et al.*, (1989). They suggest that children with 'avoidant-insecure' attachment relationships lack trust and expect hostility, and may thus develop aggressive patterns of interaction with peers. By contrast, children with 'ambivalent-avoidant' attachment relationships with parents are likely to be getting haphazard care and doubt their own effectiveness in influencing the caregiver. While staying somewhat dependent, they lack self-esteem and confidence in their own worth; and are thus susceptible to being victimized by peers.

Rubin *et al.* (1990) extend this idea and propose a more complex model, or set of developmental pathways, linking familial circumstances, infant temperament, mother–infant attachment, child-rearing techniques, self-esteem, and peer relationships. However they also postulate two main pathways, one leading to aggressive or provocative peer problems, the other leading to more passive/ withdrawal problems and difficulties in initiating and maintaining relationships. The latter is linked to dispositional/temperamental traits in the child such as shyness, behavioural reticence or behavioural inhibition; and to insecure attachment patterns; leading to anxiety, lack of social success, and further withdrawal. This is perceived by potential bullies who then select the individual as their victim. These experiences lower the individual's self-esteem, which further marks them out as an easy victim in the peer group. A vicious cycle can then be set up, reinforced by the child's reputation in the peer group.

This latter approach does not put so much emphasis on social skills, as on dispositional factors in the child, and the child's model of relationships. However, social withdrawal will in itself lead to less practice in important peer social skills; so many withdrawn children, and many victims, may indeed lack some skills, even if this may not be a primary cause for their condition.

Intervention strategies

A lot can be done to reduce bully/victim problems in schools, and there is now considerable evidence that interventions can be effective. The most extensive intervention has been carried out in Norway. National concern peaked following one week in 1982 when two children separately committed suicide because of bullying. A nationwide intervention campaign was started, with the backing of the Ministry of Education, in 1983. A resource pack, consisting of a videotape for class discussion, a booklet for teachers, and a folder of advice for parents, was provided for (and to varying extents used by) every middle and secondary school in the country.

An evaluation by Olweus in the Bergen area on 42 schools, used a cohort-sequential design, starting with 11–14 year olds in 1983, and using exactly the same testing procedures at three time points (1983/84/85). The design enables comparisons of same-age children who have, or have not, experienced the intervention to various extents. The results show a clear and marked decrease (for both boys and girls) in reports of being bullied, bullying others, and of antisocial behaviour generally; and an increase in reported liking of school. The effects on self-reported bullying are supported by data from peer nominations. The reported level of bullying was found to decrease by around 50 per cent. This important finding suggests that a properly funded national intervention campaign can have a marked and successful impact.

Other countries, notably the USA and Japan, are developing programmes related to bullying in schools. Based on the Elton Report and widespread concern about the issue, the DES is funding a follow-up to the Sheffield survey service, enabling us to assist 21 schools in their intervention policies, monitor their implementation, and assess their effectiveness.

The Sheffield Project is evaluating a range of interventions. All the schools taking part are working on a whole-school approach to the problem. In addition, some schools are using curricular interventions, such as use of video or drama or story and role-play techniques. Some are involving children in problem solving and decision making through regular participation in quality circles. Other interventions work particularly on relationships between pupils.

One such method, based on the social skills model, is to provide victims with appropriate skills of assertiveness, joining in groups, co-operation and sharing. The skills can also be taught directly. For a review of social skills work with victims of bullying, see Arora (1991). We are currently looking at co-operative group work techniques in the classroom as a way of improving social relationships (Smith, et al., 1989; Cowie and Rudduck, 1991). In this way, children are helped and encouraged to work together on common tasks, sharing experiences, and dealing with difficulties and conflicts in relationships (with the help of the teacher) as they arise. So far, this looks like being a helpful technique both in integrating children into the peer group, and reducing problems of bullying.

An approach which may be useful for cases of group bullying, or 'mobbing', is the 'Method of Shared Concern' advocated by Pikas (1989). Here, children involved in group bullying are seen individually and some degree of concern for the predicament of the victim is elicited. The child is asked for suggestions as to what can be done, and the adult arranges to see them again the following week to see how things are progressing. The adult may also see the victim, and if necessary arrange a meeting between the bullies and the victim once matters have progressed satisfactorily to a sufficient extent.

The results of the Sheffield Project will be disseminated on a national basis. In the interim, suggestions for practical action are available in Elliott (1991) and Smith and Thompson (1991). Hopefully, the next few years will see major steps being taken to improve pupil relationships and reduce bullying during a child's years at school.

ACKNOWLEDGEMENTS

We are grateful to the ESRC (Swindon) and the Gulbenkian Foundation (London) for their financial support, and to Irene Whitney for the survey results.

REFERENCES

Ahmad, Y, Whitney, I and Smith, PK (1991) 'A survey service for schools on bully/victim problems', in Smith PK and Thompson DA (eds), *Practical Approaches to Bullying*, London: David Fulton.

Arora, CMJ (1991) The use of victim support groups, in Smith PK and Thompson DA (eds), *Practical Approaches to Bullying*, London: David Fulton.

Besag, V (1989) *Bullies and Victims in Schools*, Milton Keynes: Open University Press.

Boulton, MJ and Smith, PK (1991) Bully/victim problems in middle school children: stability, self-perceived competence, peer perceptions, and peer acceptance, Manuscript submitted for publication.

Bowlby, J (1988) *A Secure Base: Clinical Applications of Attachment Theory*, London: Tavistock/Routledge.

Burnage Report (1989) *Murder in the Playground*, London: Longsight Press.

Coie, JD Dodge, KA and Coppotelli, HA (1982) Dimensions and types of social status: A cross-age perspective, *Developmental Psychology*, **18**, 557–69.

Cowie, H and Rudduck, J (1991) *Co-operative Group Work in the Multi-ethnic Classroom. Learning Together, Working Together*, Volume Four, London: BP Educational Service.

DES (1989) *Discipline in Schools*, (The Elton Report) London: HMSO.

Dodge, KA, Pettit, GS, McClaskey, CL and Brown MM (1986). Social competence in children, *Monographs of the Society for Research in Child Development*, **51**(2), 1–85.

Elliott, M (ed.) (1991) *Bullying: A Practical Guide to Coping for Schools*, Harlow: Longman.

Gilmartin, BG (1987) Peer group antecedents of severe love-shyness in males, *Journal of Personality*, **55**, 467–89.

Lane, D (1989) Violent histories: bullying and criminality, in Tattum DP and Lane DA (eds), *Bullying in Schools*, Stoke-on-Trent: Trentham Books.

Lesser, GS (1959) The relationship between various forms of aggression and popularity among lower-class children, *Journal of Educational Psychology*, **50**, 20–25.

Mellor, A (1990) Bullying in Scottish secondary schools, *Spotlights 23*, Edinburgh: SCRE.

O'Moore, AM and Hillery, B (1989) Bullying in Dublin schools, *Irish Journal of Psychology*, **10**, 426–41.

Olweus, D (1978) *Aggression in the Schools: Bullies and Whipping Boys*, Washington, DC: Hemisphere.

Olweus, D (1989) Bully/victim problems among schoolchildren: basic facts and effects of a school based intervention program, in Rubin K and Pepler D (eds), *The Development and Treatment of Childhood Aggression*, Hillsdale, NJ: Erlbaum.

Parker, JG and Asher, SR (1987) Peer relations and later personal adjustment: are low-accepted children at risk?, *Psychological Bulletin*, **102**, 357–89.

Perry, DG, Kusel, SJ and Perry, LC (1988) Victims of peer aggression, *Developmental Psychology*, **24**, 807–14.

Pikas, A (1989) The Common Concern Method for the treatment of Mobbing, in Roland E and Munthe E (eds), *Bullying: an International Perspective*, London: David Fulton.

Renken, B, Egeland, B, Marvinney, D, Mangelsdorf, S and Sroufe, LA (1989) Early childhood antecedents of aggression and passive-withdrawal in early elementary school, *Journal of Personality*, **57**, 257–81.

Robins, LN (1986) The consequences of conduct disorder in girls, in Olweus, D, Block, J and Radke-Yarrow, M (eds), *Development of Antisocial and Prosocial Behavior: Research, Theories and Issues*, New York: Academic Press.

Roland, E and Munthe, E (eds) (1989) *Bullying: an International Perspective*, London: David Fulton.

Rubin, KH, LeMare, LJ and Lollis, S (1990) Social withdrawal in childhood: Developmental pathways to peer rejection, in Asher SR and Coie JD (eds), *Peer Rejection in Childhood*, Cambridge: Cambridge University Press.

Rutter, M (1989) Pathways from childhood to adult life, *Journal of Child Psychology and Psychiatry*, **30**, 23–51.

Smith, PK (1991) The silent nightmare: bullying and victimisation in school peer groups, *The Psychologist*, **4**, 243–8.

Smith, PK, Boulton, M and Cowie, H (1989) Ethnic relations in middle school, Final Report to ESRC, Swindon.

Smith, PK and Thompson, DA (eds) (1991) *Practical Approaches to Bullying*, London: David Fulton.

Stephenson, P and Smith, D (1989) Bullying in the junior school, in Tattum DP and Lane DA (eds), *Bullying in Schools*, Stoke-on-Trent: Trentham Books.

Tattum, DP and Lane, DA (1989) *Bullying in Schools*, Stoke-on-Trent: Trentham Books.

Troy, M and Sroufe, LA (1987) Victimisation among preschoolers: role of attachment history relationship, *Journal of American Academy of Child and Adolescent Psychiatry*, **26**, 166–72.

Whitney, I and Smith, PK (1991) A survey of the nature and extent of bullying in junior/middle and secondary schools. Manuscript submitted for publication.

Part Three: Learning Through Curriculum Initiatives

Chapter 6

Curriculum Initiatives and Pupil Achievement in Oxfordshire

Neville Jones and Eileen Baglin Jones

INTRODUCTION

In July 1982, the Secretary of State for Education, Sir Keith Joseph (now Lord Joseph), launched the Lower Attaining Pupils Programme (LAPP), the first major national curriculum to be managed directly by the Department of Education and Science. The aims of the LAP Programme were:

- to improve the educational attainment of pupils mainly in years four and five, (years 10 and 11 in the National Curriculum) for whom existing examinations at 16 plus were not designed, and who were not benefiting fully from school; and
- to shift education away from a narrowly conceived or inappropriate curriculum provision and teaching styles to approaches more suited to the needs of pupils. To give a practical slant to much of what was taught. To prepare pupils better for the satisfactions and obligations of adult life and the world of work, and to improve their self-respect and motivation.

A sum of £2 million per year was provided by the government from September 1983: provided out of the Urban Aid Programme (Department of the Environment), and inflation linked. Each LEA whose project proposal was successful had to provide 25 per cent of the cost from its own resources. Some 17 widely differing LAPP projects were in operation by 1986. The grants received by LEAs ranged from £70,000 to £700,000. This diversity of funding was also reflected in the different ways in which individual LEAs launched their projects: some through centralized curriculum initiatives, others through school based developments. None of the LEAs used the title 'LAPP' in their initiatives, and in the Oxfordshire initiative, which is the account given in this chapter, the title adopted was the 'New Learning Initiative' (NLI). The focus of the national projects was on different parts of the curriculum in respective LEAs: these ranged from a whole curriculum approach to projects that centred down on specific aspects of learning, for example, linking the project to the National Oracy Programme and competence in speaking and learning (Tann, 1990); utilizing Feuerstein's (1980) *Instrumental Enrichment* which is a cognitive skills development scheme (Bray, 1992), and projects aimed at improving pupil performance in basic subjects like maths, English and science.

The LEAs were recommended to appoint their own evaluators (for example Leeson, 1989) and projects were evaluated by the National Foundation for Educational Research (NFER) (see Further Reading at the end of this chapter for an extended list of publications by the NFER and Oxfordshire County Council). Her Majesty's Inspectorate evaluated the projects for the period 1984-5 (DES, 1986) and again for the period 1982-88 (DES, 1989). Assessment and evaluation, together with a wider perspective of the issues arising from the LAP programme, have in recent years been the topics covered by commentators (Harland and Weston, 1987; Leeson, *et al.*, 1988; Nash, 1987).

Since the raising of the school leaving age in 1973 there had been a growing concern for the education of lower attaining pupils. A number of reports (*Aspects of Secondary Education*, 1979; DES 1984) all reported that:

> the curriculum of such pupils was frequently narrow, undemanding, lacking in coherence and seldom pitched at a level which demanded worthwhile achievement.
> . . . course objectives were often unclear, or when clear, often inappropriate, and expectations were frequently unduly low among both pupils and staff.

In March 1985 the government published a White Paper, *Better Schools*, which was to be part of an effort to 'raise expectations and improve the attainment of pupils at all levels of ability' and to investigate 'how differentiation is best developed and applied across the curriculum for pupils within the chosen target groups' (DES 1986). At that time the government was anticipating the introduction of General Certification of Secondary Education with targets for a wider range of pupils. HMI had suggested 'that the aims [of LAPP] might be achieved principally through a shift in teaching styles and curricular provision of approaches more suited to the pupils' needs and that those needs should themselves be more accurately diagnosed (DES, 1989). It was recognized that the pupils to be targeted could not be regarded as a homogeneous group and it was not possible to phase them in strict and rigid categories. It was the government's view that in some respect low attainers required an alternative curriculum but within the social framework of the rest of a school: it would be a curriculum that included work schemes, community projects and pupil profiles. A consequence of this was that in a number of schools LAPP became an isolated exercise, seen as no more than a skills (without education) training initiative, and having little influence on the main curriculum with its subject/examination orientation. A further concern was teachers' attitudes to a programme of this kind. Some had expressed the opinion that LAPP further marginalized a group of pupils who had already become disaffected with their schooling experience. There was the risk that pupils at this stage in education might become regarded as slow and special, requiring an education removed from the main-stream coursework options. To avoid this Hargreaves (1984) had earlier suggested that the final two years of compulsory education should be limited on coursework lines, and in one Oxfordshire comprehensive school, where the whole of the curriculum was modular, LAPP became an additional option available to *all* pupils. With a strong residential component the school found this module attractive to its slow learning pupils.

Curriculum initiatives in Oxfordshire, set in train in the 1980s were aimed not only at addressing the needs of those in the 14–16 year age group, and for the most part slow-learning, but also at determining what styles of LEA and school management, what teaching strategies and appropriate curriculum (all within a context and school ethos of positive learning experiences for all) would enhance the schooling experience of all pupils. In this chapter we will look at three of these initiatives: one originating with central government directives and funding, and two arising from the LEA initiatives. These were, respectively, the *New Learning Initiative* (NLI) translated directly from the government's Lower Attaining Pupil Project; the LEA projected *Achievement Project* (AP); and the *Disaffected Pupil Programme* (DPP).

THE NEW LEARNING INITIATIVE

The initial problem facing teachers in Oxfordshire schools was the critical one of how to plan and execute an effective curriculum for pupils of possibly low motivation, poor self-esteem, and whose expectations for gaining meaningful employment on leaving school were low. The targeting of the NLI programme so specifically in one sense tied the hands of the teachers: many felt that the seeds of low attainment which would so frequently manifest themselves in disturbed behaviour patterns, were sown much earlier than age 14. Oxfordshire teachers attempted to identify, through check-lists, discussions with pupils, teacher observations, test and examination results and discussion with parents, areas of difficulty in terms of motivation, behaviour, aptitude and performance. The issue was complex: it was difficult to separate out the strands and determine the sources or influences that gave rise to low achievement and poor behaviour. Some schools fell into the trap of attempting to identify individual pupils with the aim of providing an alternative curriculum: a process which only emphasized the lack of achievement and confirmed for some pupils the low opinion of themselves. In this approach the changes brought about were not seen as the responsibility of all staff nor did the changes really challenge teachers', parents' and pupils' fixed notions of ability and achievement. Such pupils soon became sink groups. It was a question of teachers feeling their way forward and learning as the project progressed, facilitated by a team of community-link tutors and a co-ordinator with responsibility for the evaluation of the project.

The idea of a community-link tutor post, which involved schools using teachers in an enabling, supportive non-teaching role, was an unfamiliar one at the beginning of the NLI project. There were the familiar problems of change introduced to institutions that have a regularity of practice: roles are unclear; the credibility of the tutors; the need to explore objectives, methods and purposes. This on-going process of appraisal and adjustment for the tutors determined how effective these posts proved to be and the extent to which schools could effectively develop curriculum-based community programmes.

The resources of the project were eventually channelled into three main activities:

(a) school-community links;
(b) instrumental enrichment; and
(c) residential education.

School-community links

The school-community links part of the project which aimed to provide pupils with different and more motivating contexts for learning proved to be a very successful part of the NLI project. Examples of community links were placements in primary schools, playgroups, hospitals, old people's centres, libraries, charity shops, and assistance with Meals on Wheels. Pupils were engaged in painting and decorating, designing and making toys, producing community newsletters, and fundraising. The community-link schemes also involved adults coming into the school to share their knowledge and skills; for example career officers, youth workers, parents, artists and first aid course leaders.

Instrumental enrichment

A second strand in the Oxfordshire NLI programme was the introduction of Feuerstein's (1980) scheme called *Instrumental Enrichment*: a scheme involving the teacher in intensive verbal mediation in pupil learning and focusing on pencil-and-paper problem-solving exercises to improve the intellectual functioning of the pupils concerned. The scheme claims to make a radical and permanent improvement in the cognitive funtioning of low-performing pupils: it offers teachers a powerful tool to affect underachievement. In the context of the New Learning Initiative programme it has been used as part of a general enrichment for pupils. The Feuerstein programme of work was extended in Oxfordshire and became known as the *Oxfordshire Skills Programme*.

Residential education

This part of the NLI initiative aimed to explore how residential education could become an integral part of curricular provision, with appropriate preparation and follow-up: it was seen as an important aspect of social education.

Several of the aims and objectives of the NLI project could be met readily by the provision of residential experience and included:

- changing concepts of success and achievement;
- providing different contexts for learning;
- improving pupils' relationships with the school;
- widening pupil horizons; and
- promoting social and personal skills.

The activities covered by the Residential Experience programme included: using the facilities of the four residential centres belonging to the Oxfordshire County Council; using the Youth Hostel service; camping, canoeing, sailing, skiing, running arts courses; the setting up of a business studies group; expeditions to the Forest of Dean, the Brecon Beacons and Exmoor National Park; courses in survival and self-reliance; and visits to four of the First World War battlefields.

Initially it was self-evident that both pupils and teachers regarded the activities as successful in pursuing the aims of the project, improving pupil motivation and raising standards of work. The perceptions were tested in due course, with the development of more skills of analysis, giving rise to issues that had relevance not only to the NLI group but to pupils in general.

The critical question about the learning of lower-achieving pupils is how to make it an experience characterized by success and achievement rather than failure and reluctance to learn.

One of the most obvious concerns of the NLI project has been the need to make learning more immediate and personalized – more able to cater for the needs of the individual pupil, more likely to make the individual valued and actively involved. Residential education has been one of the most obvious and available ways in which these qualities have been realized for many pupils in the project.

For this reason residential education focused the thinking in the NLI project on issues which then needed to be considered in terms of the whole school's policy and practice in many areas, e.g. in social education, pupil profiling, pastoral care, practical work in science and the humanities, and in creating opportunities for independent learning. While there has been a long tradition of outdoor education and a recognized value attached to the particular kinds of learning experience it provides, residential education is now seen as a more important part of a curriculum which recognizes a broad range of achievements and gives a central place to the issue of personal and social education – of *all* pupils. Schools were challenged not to regard some form of residential experience as an optional extra and only for some pupils.

The notion of social and personal education implies some elements of direct and active experience with others in a range of contexts. Also the question of achievement cannot be tackled seriously, as the NLI project has demonstrated, without a willingness on the part of schools to look at their organization and ethos, their methods and forms of delivery, and the quality of pupil-teacher relationships and pastoral care; and to expand the curriculum to include a wider range of opportunities for success for pupils. Among the criteria for success for pupils' learning in many contexts would be their increased powers of communication and self-awareness, interest and enthusiasm, and their confidence in their abilities and trust in their teachers. These are social and personal gains from and ingredients in the learning process which schools aim to provide and foster and which have been made more and more explicit in the shape of social and personal education courses, residential work, counselling, profiling and work experience. Residential education, therefore, has come to be viewed as a significant vehicle for, and part of, social education and a learning opportunity which may be cross-curricular and subject focused in a number of different ways.

In spite of the financial constraints, many schools are now keen that all pupils should have at least one kind of residential experience in which, no matter what the curriculum content, there would be a recognized emphasis on the pupils' social and personal development. This often takes place as part of a tutorial programme or a social education course and helps to locate residential work within the mainstream curriculum. One area of difficulty for schools in the NLI project was to organize residential experience in a clearly worked out curriculum context rather than as a bolt-on extra. Further work in the project led to greater expertise among many subject teachers to plan and integrate residential education into a number of curriculum areas, and to provide better continuity and progression between learning which takes place in the classroom and on residential course. An important outcome of this part of the NLI project was that some of the schools involved now have a better co-ordinated programme for all residential work and a clearer policy on this aspect of education. These are the schools which are now willing to devote more resources to residential work and which plan its location in the mainstream curriculum.

The *advantages* of this approach are:

1. More monitoring of pupils' out-of-school learning experiences.
2. Specific criteria for the planning and selection of pupils for particular kinds of residential experience.
3. Residentials are not seen as one-off experiences but as more integrated with other kinds of learning.
4. Teachers build on their experience and develop new expertise in this area.
5. Social education has wider scope and contains more elements of active experimental learning.
6. Cross-curricular work is encouraged and can be planned for.
7. More evidence of what pupils can do is more easily available to teachers, to aid profiling and to enhance pupil–teacher relationships.
8. Parental contact and involvement is often increased.
9. Pupils become more involved in planning and appraising their own programmes of learning.
10. The school's organization and timetabling frequently become more flexible.

There are also many *difficulties* involved in a greater emphasis on, and more provision of, residential work:

1. In many schools residential trips present great disruption to the school's timetabling and staffing.
2. The mechanisms do not exist for organizing and utilizing the learning on residential courses in an integrated way with other parts of the curriculum, or in a cross-curricular way.
3. Staff time and commitment may be a problem, especially now in connection with the new conditions of service and 'directed' time.
4. Only certain staff will have the necessary interest and skills for residential courses.
5. With the lack of central funding the financial resources for

residential work often mean a radical review of the school's priorities for capitation money, and inevitably in more cases some parental contribution.

6. Some pupils – in many cases those most lacking in confidence and social skills – are reluctant to go on residential trips.

7. In an overtly 'academic' ethos residential education may be too easily associated only with field study in certain subjects or with 'trips out' for the 'less able'.

8. There is often a lack of in-service training support for residential work, although the NLI project has done a lot in this area.

9. Some schools complain about the lack of LEA and central government policy and funding for residential education, and as a result respond less readily to develop their provision.

Major initiatives such as the TVEI Extension, the NLI Project, some aspects of GCSE, and even some of the government's questionable plans to look at the ethos of schools and the social behaviour of pupils as indicators of performance, throw the spotlight on residential education and the kinds of learning opportunities it provides. There is an urgent need for clearly articulated school and LEA policy, for a review of the critical issues to do with funding and pupil selection for, and entitlement to, this kind of education opportunity.

Teachers in the NLI referred continually to the residential work in the project as the most obvious and dramatic vehicle for changing pupils' attitudes to learning, increasing motivation and self-esteem, and creating opportunities for some of the most significant positive achievements for pupils with a history of failure. Similarly pupils quote their residential experiences as some of the most memorable learning experiences they have had, and interestingly, show considerable ability to analyse and be critical of themselves as learners in those situations.

Some of the most noticeable remarks made by other teachers about pupils in the NLI project refer to their attitudes and behaviour and general demeanour. These qualities – in some schools quite a a dramatic change of ethos among fifth year learners – arise out of the central emphasis in the NLI project on pupil–teacher relationships and more collaborative and pupil-centred modes of learning. This emphasis is epitomized in the project's focus on residential education.

A certain amount of criticism is justified for some of the delivery and organization of residential work in the project. Some was badly planned, poorly organized, lacked meaningful learning connections with school-based work and failed to provide follow up work and useful extension for pupils. Some relied too heavily on 'packaged' county residential centre-based courses when other kinds of provision might have been constrained by inflexible organizational arrangements and lack of LEA support especially in terms of supply cover for teachers. Like any major piece of curriculum development the NLI project experimented and explored, quite widely, the possibilities of residential work, so that schools are now in a position to consolidate, support, make recommendations and disseminate good practice.

THE ACHIEVEMENT PROJECT

The good practice developed by the NLI project in managerial support to schools, relevance to appropriate curriculum, and project style, encouraged the Oxfordshire County Council to fund a further development project, known as the Achievement Project, as a successor to the NLI project. The lessons learned and the skills developed through the NLI project allowed for further commitment to the work to test its application to a broader spectrum of pupils in mainstream schools.

Different groups of schools moved into the Project which challenged mainstream teaching staff to identify areas of under-achievement and demanded strategies to overcome them. The emphasis was on school-based curriculum development. Four community-link tutors facilitated the partnership between a small central team and teachers in the schools. LAPP, being the first major attempt by the government to address the problem of pupil disaffection, and hence all the problems of misbehaviour and discipline, brought about a shift in attitudes and practice on the part of teachers. Among the gains is perhaps that of disaffected pupils becoming aware that their school experience could have a relevance according to their needs and abilities. The critical balance between behaviour and pupil achievement, where pupil energies are increasingly towards misbehaviour and away from success in curriculum matters for the disaffected pupil, is slowly re-adjusted as behavioural energies become focused on improvement in school work. LAPP, reflected in the New Learning Initiative and Achievement projects in Oxfordshire, created a major reform for meeting individual needs but in reality had a much wider impact in terms of pupil self–esteem, learning and accomplishment, with a consequence of having something to say about behaviour and discipline in schools. This was an area of the 'schools discipline' issue which needed far more research and thinking about at the time the Elton committee was holding its deliberations. Where pupils felt valued and were succeeding in their school work (and importantly, there is a legitimate place for these particular skills and knowledge) such pupils are less inclined to behave in ways that were beginning to give concern to some teacher unions. The essence of LAPP was in focusing attention on how schools could make an effective *curriculum* response to certain pupils within a framework of a whole-school policy. The problems that brought about the refocusing continue in schools, and are likely to do so for some time. Whatever pre-occupation teachers have in incorporating the requirements of the 1988 Education Reform Act, it has yet to be seen how far matters like the management of the National Curriculum can be extended, through government prompting or local school initiative, to incorporate the lessons learned through LAPP. At some stage the *pupil* will need to be re-instated as the focus of a school's activities rather than the minutiae of matters relating to the management of schools and the publicizing of the curriculum for all pupils in state schools. The issue of school discipline is one of effective school management and appropriate curriculum: so far the efforts by government through its legislation have been to focus attention on aspects of school management and curriculum planning that have certain political outcomes, and it is feared that such strategies have more to do with marginalizing pupils in more systematic bureaucratic structures than in attempts, as made through such measures as LAPP, to meet pupil needs wherever they are found.

THE DISAFFECTED PUPIL PROGRAMME

A third strand in the Oxfordshire initiative to meet the needs of underachieving pupils, whether because of lower ability, emotional needs or response to the education they were experiencing, was the setting up of the Disaffected Pupil Programme. This project had a quite different focus compared with work being carried out through the NLI and Achievement Project activities. At the time of its commencement teachers were still recovering from their confrontational strike with the government, and in fact, the government was already focusing the blame for hooliganism in the wider society on what was happening in our schools. Teachers were yet again being set-up as scape-goats for all that was seen as bad and going wrong in Britain: the outcome, because, it was said, of school practices, was more disaffected, disruptive and delinquent young people than ever before. The cause for teachers was taken up by at least one teacher union who supported the view that schools in Britain were 'seas of chaos'. All this led to an HMI investigation into school discipline, and later, the setting up of the Elton Committee. The reports by both these authoritative bodies did not support the contentions of politicians and a growing body of teachers that chaos was reigning in our schools. There were clearly some schools where discipline was a problem and pupils were disaffected with their school experiences and with themselves. HMI had in 1988 published a report, *Secondary Schools: An Appraisal by HMI*, to the effect, 'the behaviour of pupils was often extremely good and they were generally co-operative.

In only a very small number of schools (5 per cent) were substantial difficulties being experienced in the classroom' (para. 29). The report had followed on from HMI the previous year where a small team of HMI had looked specifically at behaviour and discipline in schools, (Behaviour and Discipline in School – Education Observed 5) and found that violence of a significant nature was a limited phenomenon in schools. The HMI reports together with the Elton Report were not good news for a government determined to attack and demoralize the teaching profession: it is not surprising that the enormous amount of research and professional opinion reviewed in the Elton Report found little recognition in the terms of the 1988 Education Reform Act. Pupil behaviour was treated in the Act as a quite separate and distinctive issue from the main thrust of the reform, reflecting a discontinuity between government policy and developments that had been taking place in schools during the 1980s.

Those working in, and supporting, schools in Oxfordshire were not aware of the excesses claimed for pupil behaviour elsewhere in the country, particularly in large urban areas. There was, in Oxfordshire, plenty of evidence of good management, innovative teaching, and the planning of appropriate curriculum. Schools were exploring ideas about whole-school philosophies and practice and the integration into mainstream schools of pupils with special needs was becoming a central plank for school policy-making. This was not to deny that Oxfordshire schools had disruptive pupils, had reason to be concerned with underachievement, and had its quota of disaffected in the school population. In the post-Warnock Report era, a survey of all pupils in the Banbury area was carried out by the County School Psychological Services to determine needs and to explore the possibility that in Banbury there could be devised an ethos about pupils needs, i.e. all pupils, irrespective of individual needs would be on the roll of ordinary schools and treated as normal members of the school and wider community. The survey revealed that pupil needs in the area approximated to that revealed in national surveys carried out by the HMI and the Elton Committee. It also revealed that where good practice was pursued there was considerable difficulty in having this disseminated – a problem not unique to schools in Oxfordshire but affecting the education service in Britain as a whole.

The overall aim of the Disaffected Pupil Programme was, therefore, to discover in Oxfordshire schools, and elsewhere, good practice in school management, teaching and curriculum planning, that in outcome would prevent pupils becoming disaffected, or would provide the means for rehabilitating pupils in need of this kind without resource to marginalizing practice, such as the utilization of special units, classes or schools, but within a framework of whole-school management and participation. The first task was to identify where good practice was taking place, through official reports and research surveys, through the professional journals, through the media, and through recognized educational networks. The next step was to engage in dialogue with those engaged in such work, and this meant in many cases, contacting teachers and support services who were not necessarily part of recognized government or LEA designated projects like the LAPP scheme. An important part of this contact was to convince teachers that they had the skills, some to be developed through the Project, to write about their thinking, practice and the extent to which they would have had to modify their work in the light of experience gained. It was a tactical part of the Project to collate the material and to bring it to publication.

The Project aimed at engaging with disaffection in the education system in three ways. First, to explore how disaffection revealed itself at the different phases in the education system. What were the characteristics of the phenomenon as pupils progressed from primary to secondary schools? At each stage the needs of pupils are clearly different, but also the challenges they face in their schooling are dependent on what kind of educational structure and organization they find themselves in, and not least, what expectations there are for learning and behaviour. The material on school management and strategies for teaching, aimed at identifying or preventing disaffection, i.e. good practice in effective schools, was collated to provide four publications. It was hoped that from this strategy it would be possible to see how disaffection either began as an experience in infant education and steadily became worse as pupils worked their way through the educational system, or how in different phases, certain pupils slotted in and became part of the school's disaffected population. Disaffection at infant school level was covered by a volume called *Disaffection from School? The Early Years* (Barrett, 1989). The problems of disaffection in the junior school were covered by a volume called *Education and Alienation in the Junior School* (edited by Jim Docking, formerly Principal Lecturer in Education at the Roehampton Institute of Education, London) published in 1990. The volume on disaffection in secondary education was linked in with the work being carried out by the Elton Committee on school discipline. The volume called *School Management and Pupil Behaviour* (edited by Neville Jones, then Principal Educational Psychologist for Oxfordshire) was published in 1989. An important contribution to the series was a volume devoted to students in further education called *Uneasy Transitions* (edited by Jenny Corbett of the Open University) published in 1990. Pupils in mainstream schools who were already identified as having special educational needs were also covered in a set of three publications under the title of *Special Educational Needs Review*, Vols 1–3 (edited by Neville Jones, 1989–90), and covered much of the innovatory work that was being carried out for a particular population of mainstream pupils in the 1980s. Additionally, the Project looked at three other areas related to pupil needs in ordinary schools: a volume on *Needs, Rights and Opportunities*, edited by Caroline Roaf and Hazel Bines, and published in 1989; a volume on *Consultancy in the United Kingdom* edited by Carol Aubrey, and published in 1990; and a volume called *Refocusing Educational Psychology*, edited by Neville Jones and Norah Frederickson, published in 1990. This latter book was a follow-on from an earlier publication (*Management and the Psychology of Schooling*, edited by Neville Jones and John Sayer) which looked at issues relating to how educational psychology could more effectively be utilized in the education services.

DISCUSSION

Good educational practice, its nature and methods of delivery, were the main focus of all the projects described in this chapter: the New Learning Initiative and Achievement Project, as well as the Disaffected Pupil Programme. The AP extended the dialogue and practice beyond a small selected group of pupils at the top end of secondary education. The Disaffected Pupil Programme extended tl e issue still further: into all phases of education, into areas of special need, consultancy and school psychology. This is part of the legacy of education innovation in the 1980s. In the present decade the emphasis has switched to matters of management and structure: changes in the roles of governing bodies and the powers and rights of parents; schemes for opting out and open enrolment; new methods in teacher training; and a National Curriculum with targets and league tables. Hargreaves (1989) made reference to the remarks of Mary Warnock who in her 1988 Ian Ramsey lecture in Oxford, pointed out that:

> the creation of an education reform is a good time to reconsider the moral principles that lie behind educational policy and to allow the principles to shine through, illuminating and explaining what was wrong before and what will be put right in the future.

Hargreaves goes on to comment:

> Whatever the merits and demerits of the 1988 Reform Act, there is little doubt that, in comparison with the 1944 Act, it seems to lack any great moral purpose of connection. Its underlying philosophy derives from the principles of competitive individualism and consumer rights. There is nothing to add to or enhance our view of schools as moral communities, educating the young for rational autonomy and social inter-

dependence, along with academic achievement and preparation for working life.

It has yet to be seen whether the innovations of the 1980s, geared specifically to the needs of pupils, are just the other side of the coin of innovation deriving from the 1988 Education Reform Act. There is no guarantee so far that we are involved with a common currency, even though teachers have to bridge the divide between pupil needs and political considerations.

The three curriculum initiatives outlined above were not the only projects that were beginning to get off the ground in the 1980s. Additionally, work was progressing with the Oxfordshire Examinations Syndicate Credit Bank, which was funded by Oxfordshire County Council, and which together with the Southern Examination Group developed and piloted Modular Mode III GCSE courses. Also, of particular importance were the two initiatives concerned with the assessment and recording of achievement: one being the Oxford Certificate of Education Achievement (OCEA) arising in the context of secondary education, and the other, the Assessment, Profiling and Reporting programme (APR) at primary level.

Each of these projects supported three certain general aims which the LEA had identified in considering the role of schools. The aims were:

(1) to promote the self-development of children so that they are able on leaving formal education to be active, responsible, confident, independent and contributing members of society;
(2) to enhance children's skills, knowledge, experience, imagination, appreciation and moral awareness;
(3) to keep under regular review and refine through self-appraisal the school's own practices.

In successfully pursuing these aims schools took account of a number of factors which include:

- the recognition of, and provision for, individual needs;
- learning methods and resources which encourage success rather than failure, initiative and imagination rather than inhibition, motivation rather than lethargy;
- the need for continuity and progression in learning, both within schools and at transfer;
- the need to keep a positive record of children's achievements, to which they and their parents will contribute.

If there has been one overriding concern expressed through the projects and initiatives described above, whether through improved management, skilled and innovative teaching, appropriate curriculum for all, and a whole-school ethos, it is that pupils can look back on their school days with a sense of achievement. Whatever strategies are employed in the classroom to cope, or to suppress or otherwise deflect individual incidents of inapppro- priate behaviour on the part of students, the long-term strategy for substantial change must come about through an effective and meaningful curriculum. The chapters in this part of the book draw attention to some of these initiatives in curriculum management which already have had a pay-off in many schools and in the self- esteem of many pupils. The main thrust of the 'School discipline' issue must be along these lines, no matter how many false starts, how much frustration, and how much trial and error is expended in seeking goals and solutions that make for an effective school, meeting needs wherever they arise, for adults as well as pupils.

FURTHER READING

The following are publications arising from the Oxfordshire 'New Learning Initiative' project

A. Newsletters Nos 1–16

B. Occasional Papers:

No. 1 *Issues for Development and Dissemination*
No. 2 *In-service Training and Staff Development*
No. 3 *A Focus On: Open and Interactive Learning*
No. 4 *School-Community Links and Experimental Learning*
No. 5 *A Focus On: School-Community Links*
No. 6 *Identifying Lower Attaining Pupils*
No. 7 *Teaching Cognitive Skills*
No. 8 *Residential Education*

C. Additional Papers:

Patrick Leeson (1985) *Instrumental Enrichment*
Eileen Baglin (1985) *Pupil Attitudes*
Pam Henderson (1985) *Residential Education*
Mick Hawes (1986) *The Use of Adults from the Community*
Trish Taylor (1986) *Taking Learning Out of the Classroom*
Rickard Elks (1986) *School-Community Links and the Achievement Curriculum*
John Fox (1986) *The Parent Community*
Tony Kelly (1986) *School-Community Links and Residential Work*
John Hanson (1987) *Oxfordshire Skills Programme*
John Hanson, Trish Taylor and Wyn Bray (1987) *Cognitive Skills Inventory*

The above publications may be obtained from the Curriculum Publishing Unit, Oxfordshire County Council, Cricket Road Cen- tre, Cricket Road, Oxford OX4 3DW; tel. 0865 716573.

National Foundation for Educational Research publications

1. Penelope Weston *The Search for Success*
2. Monica Taylor *Relationships for Learning*
3. Robert Stradling *Practical Learning*
4. Penelope Weston and Clare Morgan *Learning to Learn*
5. Penelope Weston *Purposeful Learning*
6. Monica Taylor *Residentials*
7. John Harland, Robert Stradling and Orlinda Dias *Frameworks for Learning*
8. Orlinda Dias, John Harland and Penelope Weston *Professional Practice*
9. John Harland *Budgeting for Change*

REFERENCES

Aspects of Secondary Education in England(1979) London : HMSO.

Aubrey, C. (ed) (1990) *Consultancy in the UK* Education and Alienation Series, Lewes: Falmer Press.

Baglin, E (1989) 'Project work on pupil achievement: the LAP programme' in Jones, N (ed) *School Management and Pupil Behaviour*, Education and Alienation Series, Lewes: Falmer Press.

Barrett, G. (ed) (1989) *Disaffection from School: The Early Years*, Education and Alienation Series, Lewes: Falmer Press.

Corbett, J (1990) *Uneasy Transitions*, Education and Alienation Series, Lewes: Falmer Press.

Department of Education and Science (1984) *Slow Learning and Less Successful Pupils in Secondary Schools*, London: DES.

Department of Education and Science (1985) *Better Schools*, White Paper, Cmnd 9469, London: DES.

Department of Education and Science (1986) *A Survey of the Lower Attaining Pupils' Programme: The First Two Years*, London: DES.

Department of Education and Science (1987) *Education Observed 5: Good Behaviour and Discipline in Schools*, London: DES.

Department of Education and Science (1989) *The Lower Attaining Pupils' Programme 1982–88*, London: DES.

Docking, J (ed (1990) *Education and Alienation in the Junior School*, Education and Alienation Series, Lewes: Falmer Press.

Feuerstein, R (1980) *Instrumental Enrichment: An Intervention Strategy for Cognitive Modifiability*, Baltimore: University Park Press.

Hargreaves, D (1984) *Improving Secondary Schools*, London: ILEA.

Hargreave, D (1989) 'Introduction' in Jones, N (ed) *School Management and Pupil Behaviour*, Education and Alienation Series, Lewes: Falmer Press.

Harland, J and Weston, P (1987) 'LAPP: Joseph's coat of many colours', in *British Journal of Special Education* **14**, 4, December.

Her Majesty's Inspectorate (1988) *Secondary Schools: An Appraisal by HMI*, London: DES.

Jones, N (1989) *School Management and Pupil Behaviour*, Education and Alienation Series, Lewes: Falmer Press.

Jones, N (ed) (1989–90) *Special Educational Needs Review*. Vols 1–3, Lewes: Falmer Press.

Jones, N and Frederickson, N. (eds) (1990) *Refocusing Educational Psychology,* Education and Alienation Series, Lewes: Falmer Press.

Jones, N and Sayer, J (1988) *Management and the Psychology of Schooling,* Lewes: Falmer Press.

Leeson, P (1986) *School-Community Links and Experimental Learning,* NLI Occasional Paper 4, Oxfordshire County Council.

Leeson, P (1989) *NLI Project in Oxfordshire, Year 6: Review and Evaluation 1988–89,* Oxfordshire County Council.

Leeson, P, Baglin, E and Oliver, L (eds) (1988) *Perspective on the Lower Attaining Pupils' Programme,* Oxfordshire County Council.

Nash, I (1987) 'How to Avoid the Stigma of Failure', *Times Educational Supplement* 14th August, p9.

Roaf, C and Bines, H (eds) (1989) *Needs, Rights and Opportunities,* Education and Alienation Series, Lewes: Falmer Press.

Tann, S (1990) 'Language skills and pupil needs: oracy in the classroom', in Jones, N (ed) *Special Educational Needs Review,* Vol 3, Education and Alienation Series, Lewes: Falmer Press.

Chapter 7

The Lower Attaining Pupil: Seen but not Heard

Christine Hodgkinson

RAISING ATTAINMENT

The 1988 Education Reform Act (ERA) is based on the belief that attainment can be raised by controlling what is taught and the way that it is assessed. Is this what the pupils think too? Not necessarily – the pupils seem to be more interested in how learning is organized and the school environment. Investigation of pupil experience of the curriculum indicates that there is a mismatch between what pupils think will result in more effective learning and the intentions of ERA. However, as far as ERA is concerned pupils should be seen but not heard. The social order is most effectively maintained when the government and its agents define what is useful knowledge; how pupils learn is unimportant enough to be left to schools and teachers. Attainment can only be effectively raised when as much consideration is given to learning and the learner as to the content of the curriculum and assessment.

'Core subjects', 'foundation subjects', 'attainment targets', 'key stages', 'standard assessment tasks', 'teacher assessment', 'local management of schools', 'delegated budgets'.

These are just a few of the requirements of ERA which have come to dominate the working lives of those involved with secondary education. In the welter of statutory orders and government-inspired initiatives it can be easy to forget the fundamental purposes of education. Education is for and about the pupils; what they should learn, how teaching and learning should be organized and how learning can be measured. The pupils are at the heart of the process, but far less attention is directed towards finding out what motivates pupils to learn than to defining knowledge which then dictates the content of the curriculum and how that content should be assessed.

The aims of ERA and the Low Attaining Pupils' Programme (LAPP) could be said to share at least one objective – that of raising attainment. ERA is based on the belief that this is achieved by defining knowledge, i.e. what will be taught, through identification of subject-related and age-related attainment targets and through a national programme of testing at key stages which measures how pupils have progressed against stated levels of attainment. The central focus is on teaching rather than learning and attainment targets are described for the benefit of the teacher, using language which is inaccessible to the majority of pupils.

Six years prior to ERA, the LAPP was also charged with improving attainment, particularly of those pupils in Years 4 and 5 of secondary schools who were not perceived to be benefiting fully from the existing examination system. Like ERA this often involved making explicit learning targets, but here the similarity ended. The learning targets were not intended to collectively define knowledge, but to establish short-term goals which the pupils could understand and were able to achieve. They were more closely related to learning than teaching and, therefore, much of the LAPP resource was also spent in defining the circumstances in which pupils were most likely to learn and how these circumstances could be achieved.

An HMI Report (Education Observed 12, 1989) suggested that the LAPP had some success with the latter, but that this was not necessarily translated into improving attainment as measured by examinations. While it was generally agreed that the pupils' educational experience had improved, concern was expressed about coherence in the curriculum for an individual pupil, the low level of teachers' expectations and the lack of differentiation to meet identified individual needs. The ERA and the LAPP could be said to represent opposing ends of a dimension, one focusing on knowledge and what will be taught, the other on the needs of the individual learner. Neither is satisfactory by itself, therefore neither will necessarily result in improved attainment, even if an agreed definition of attainment could be reached!

Statutory orders cover the content of the curriculum and how it will be assessed, but they make no reference to how the attainment targets are to be taught. This is the sole responsibility of the school and the teacher. In teachers' attempts to stay afloat in the deluge of paper from the National Curriculum Council and the School Examinations and Assessment Council, the importance of pupils' motivation to learn is often neglected and yet it remains the single most important factor in determining attainment. I want to describe how, in one LEA, some LAPP resources were used to investigate the perspectives of pupils on their experience of school and thus help to unravel the threads of motivation and learning.

HEARING VOICES – WHY LISTEN?

Investigating the school experience of ordinary young people is a comparatively neglected area of research. Very little time and energy has been expended in consulting pupils about how they learn; teachers, parents, HMI, the DES – these are just a few of the people who know best! Conversely, much research has been devoted to exploring the views of the minority of young people, the 'oppressed', the 'deviants', the 'failures' of the educational system. The thrust of such research has been based on an assumption that, although the causes of failure are not necessarily the responsibility of the school, by listening to these pupils we can discover faults in the system which can be rectified and failure eliminated.

Implicit in such beliefs is the notion that teachers and schools define knowledge in a way which is acceptable to society and that failure is the result of pupils' lack of ability, respect or willingness to accept the 'rightness' of what is on offer. Failure is seen in terms of individual weakness not in relation to the structure of schooling and can therefore be remedied by special provision, often entailing the watering down of the curriculum rather than reorganization of teaching and learning. However, *The Great Debate* initiated by James Callaghan at Ruskin College in 1978 shifted the emphasis to a different kind of failure; that of our secondary schools to provide for the rapidly changing needs of a modern industrial society.

Schools and their curricula were now seen not only as producing individual failure, but also as not meeting the demands of a highly technological society. Failure was not limited to Mary Warnock's 'twenty per cent' or Sir Keith Joseph's 'forty percent', but now encompassed a much wider range of pupils including those who might have been expected to succeed in the traditional grammar school curriculum. Many educationalists would support the view of Widlake:

> When normal individuals show an inability to learn in school, yet are perfectly capable of learning in other situations, one should be driven to consider what aspects of the society are creating negative attitudes. . . . (Widlake, 1985)

The early 1980s saw a plethora of local and national curriculum initiatives focused on attempts to bring schooling in line both with society's needs and more importantly, with the learning needs of young people.

Many of these initiatives still concentrated on the content of the curriculum at the expense of its organization and delivery – relevance was the new watchword. Motivation would be enhanced, disaffection reduced and attainment increased providing that the knowledge on offer was relevant. This approach took no account of changing opinion about the nature of learning and the central role of the pupil in the process. Traditional learning theories saw learning as a matter of the links between stimulus and response. The teacher is the central focus providing knowledge which the pupil will absorb and assimilate. More recent thinking, described by Clough and Nixon (1989), recognizes the responsibility of the learner as well as the teacher, the importance of interaction with the learner's previous experience and the need for the learner to be able to revise and reorder learning in the light of changing circumstances.

Such views emphasize the importance of experiential and active learning, negotiation between teacher and pupil, group work and oracy – all elements of the curriculum which are to a greater or lesser extent ignored by the requirements of the ERA. The ERA controls what is learned and how it is assessed. What is not controlled, but is crucial in raising attainment is the learner's *experience* of the curriculum. Enquiry into pupil experience can throw light on the effects of teaching on learners – not just the effects on the so-called failures, but the effects on all learners. Listening to pupils' opinions about this experience requires more than a casual tuning-in. It requires informed and systematic attempts by teachers to discover whether their practice creates an environment which will truly enhance learning and thus raise attainment.

TURNING UP THE SOUND

Acknowledging the need to listen to what pupils say about school is insufficient by itself to generate a research base within which teachers can seek to improve their practice. What is necessary is the right climate to encourage teachers to find out more about the needs of individual learners and time in which to do so. The LAPP helped to provide such a climate and the resources to follow it through; what follows is a description of the kind of research that was carried out and how it affected the teachers who took part.

The challenge of listening to pupils was issued to a group of teachers at the beginning of a period of school-focused secondment funded partly from LAPP resources and the comments included in this section were made in reports written by teachers who took part in the research. From the start it was recognized that this was something different to everyday teaching, revision of lesson content or the production of teaching materials. As one teacher put it:

I was aware of the fact that I was part of a strong team of teachers, but this wasn't teaching; this was different; some of us hadn't done anything like this for a long, long time.

For some teachers it was more than just a 'long, long time', they had never conducted any school-based research or systematically made any attempt to consider the needs of learners rather than the needs of teachers.

As with any challenge, listening to pupils had to have a purpose which was perceived by the participants as being worthwhile both to themselves, and also, perhaps more importantly, to colleagues in school who had not been charged with the grave responsibility of school-focused secondment. More traditionally, INSET was seen as the provision of skills which would make teaching more effective, often through revised teaching materials produced by experts through whose mysterious offices the difficult job of teaching would be made easier. This was a long way removed from the notion of classroom teachers developing their own skills, and those of their colleagues, simply by listening to the voice of the learners.

Listening to and analysing the views of pupils is neither simple nor easy. The teachers involved were set the task of working in groups to interview pupils in a school other than their own, analysing the data collected, giving a presentation of their findings and producing a written report for the school concerned. Thus the challenge incorporated the skills of working in a team, and of presentation as well as investigation of the pupils' experience.

Working together

A team approach or school-related development is still rare in secondary schools. The fragmentation of the curriculum into subjects has tended to isolate teachers and the organization of subjects into option blocks has fostered competition rather than collaboration. The identification of compulsory core and foundation subjects in the National Curriculum may serve to reduce competition and the introduction of cross-curricular themes could increase the necessity for team work, but many teachers have yet to be convinced of the value of working with others. It is ironic that when one of the major failings of schools is said to be the inability of young people to work together, little time is spent encouraging teachers to work co-operatively. This was highlighted by a teacher who had taken part in the research when she said,

> Another aspect of this exercise I found valuable was the group work and the sharing of tasks and responsibilities. I conclude with a question. If teachers enjoy group work and feel a sense of achievement, why not pupils?

The task set for the groups of teachers necessitated a high degree of co-operation in its planning and implementation. First, the group had to agree what topics they wished to investigate with the pupils and how the interviews would be conducted. Second, they had to trust each other to contribute to a data base and then work together to make sense of what they had been told and what implications it might have for their teaching. Finally, they were dependent on each other for the quality of their presentation and the report by which their efforts would be judged by a critical audience of peers.

The seconded teachers recognized how much was to be gained from working together. They acknowledged that, even though they had worked as colleagues, sometimes for long periods, they did not really know each other. Much more could be achieved by teams working in harmony than by individuals working in isolation. The comments they made included:

I was delighted by our joint efforts in developing a plan of campaign. . . . As a group we ploughed into the work, soon developing a system and sharing out the tasks thus making the work appear less onerous.

The [teachers] met to analyse the day's work and soon came to the realization that trying to work as an individual . . . had inhibited the efficiency of the investigation. [The research] had made them realize the benefits of working as a team. But, more importantly, it had allowed them to get to know each other and to agree that they wanted to work as a team.

The importance of the lessons learned about working together was apparent in subsequent initiatives in the LAPP schools, and on a wider basis, skills of co-operation, collaboration and negotiation are essential for the success of LEA programmes for the extension of the Technical and Vocational Education Initiative (TVEI-E) and effective implementation of the National Curriculum.

Learning to listen

At first the need for teachers to listen to pupils might seem tautological in the extreme. Surely a major part of teachers' work must involve listening to those who are taught – a truism that is not necessarily true! Teachers' interactions with their pupils rarely include the opportunity simply to find out their opinion of the education they are offered. The teacher is the subject expert, an authority who is also in authority. This role is reinforced by society's view of the teacher as the holder of knowledge, the pupil the mind to be filled. Teachers think they know what they teach in their own classrooms and, in schools where communication is good, they may know what is taught in classrooms of other members of their subject discipline and may even have an overview of the content of the school's curriculum. However, this is still knowledge shared by, and exclusive to, teachers – it does not include access to the pupils' experience of that curriculum. Do teachers need to investigate that experience? Some might say not, adults know best and anyway, we all went to school: surely we know what it is like!

The teachers who took part in the exercise were asked to suspend disbelief and listen to the views of the learners. That they were favourably impressed by the pupils they interviewed is evident from the following comments:

> The students seemed to respond positively and we found them to be friendly, prepared to talk with us and each other, and to listen to the views of the group members,

and

> The pupils responded very well to us and we were all struck by their mild mannered and generally positive, although unquestioning, attitudes to the school.

Not only did the teachers listen, they enjoyed listening:

> The interview took much longer than I had expected, mainly because we enjoyed the chat about school . . . I really enjoyed the day talking to pupils in the relaxed atmosphere and different environment,

and there was little doubt that the opportunity to listen had been seen as worthwhile and as making a useful contribution to a curriculum initiative aimed at raising attainment:

> We feel that this was a particularly valuable and informative exercise and would wish to stress that as teachers we need to listen, and to listen carefully to the views, opinions and feelings of the students we teach.

The value that the teachers placed on the exercise was not just evident in what they said, it was even more apparent from what they did. They chose to invest much more of their valuable secondment time in continuing the investigation of pupils' experience. This took a variety of forms, but always involved listening to what the pupils said about school and about learning. What they heard influenced developments which subsequently took place and then they listened again to evaluate the changes they had made.

The teachers were also convinced that successful implementation of records of achievement, an important part of the LAPP programme, was dependent on improving dialogue between teachers and pupils. Knowing how to listen is crucial when pupils and teachers collaborate to produce joint statements of the pupil's progress or negotiate learning targets. The teachers had been persuaded that what the pupils said was worth listening to, theirs was a voice to be heard.

HEARING IS BELIEVING

Once they believed that the teachers really wanted to listen, the pupils had much to say about all aspects of school and learning, but running through all that they said were two dominant and, at times conflicting, themes. They emphasized the importance of qualifications, particularly for academic subjects with high status, but they also emphasized the importance of the kind of activities which took place in lessons, relationships and the learning environment. In neither circumstance was any importance attached to the content of the curriculum, a major concern of the ERA.

On the surface much that they said supported the government's view of the purposes of school; it is about acquiring knowledge as defined by mainstream society and turning this knowledge into qualifications which will give access to desirable commodities such as, a good job and income, status, material possessions. The following two extracts from the teachers' report emphasize the importance the pupils placed on this aspect of their education:

> . . . exams figured highly in their priorities and would guarantee jobs,

and

> All the pupils I interviewed said that they were at school, yes to have a reasonably good time, they liked the relaxed atmosphere and they felt that was different from other schools, but in the end it was to get qualifications leading to jobs.

Little importance was attached to what was taught, the pupils did not expect to contribute to defining the content of the curriculum. It did not matter what you learned so long as its mastery was recognized by those who control access when compulsory schooling is over. Learning was not necessarily perceived in terms of usefulness or relevance, but in terms of status and the provision of qualifications.

How much importance was attached to the content of the curriculum was often associated with the ability of the pupils interviewed and their likelihood to gain useful qualifications. Low achievers often quoted boredom and repetition of static activities as reasons for dissatisfaction with some subjects, especially when these activities were unlikely to result in recognized achievement. Evidence from research in a similar field suggests that relevance in learning is still related by lower achievers to employment as well as to personal development. This point is reinforced by a young person who took part in a survey of the opinions of leavers from Scottish schools who had not been successful in the traditional examination system:

> I think they shouldn't give you subjects like history, geography, science etc. they might be quite interesting to some people, I liked history at school, but they are not practical and do not prepare you for life outside school; I think you should be prepared for looking for jobs. . . . (Hughes, 1984)

The beliefs which have resulted in the ERA are based on the importance of defining what is taught – the teacher is central to the process not the learner. Attainment can only be raised if content is clearly defined, but there is a tension between this view and that of the learners who attached little importance to content and much more to end-product in the form of recognition of achievement.

There is, however, a second theme which is apparent from listening to pupils and this has little to do with relevance or qualifications. A clue to this strand is given in this excerpt from a teachers' report of the pupil interviews:

> . . . the pupils were generally enthusiastic about their teachers and it is evident that the personality of the teacher and the activity involved in the lesson is more important than the nature of the subject itself.

It was evident from the interviews that the pupils were very concerned with other aspects of the learning and school. This included not only what happened in lessons, but also the provision for lunchtimes and breaks. When pupils were asked what improvements could be made to school their suggestions included:

buses to transport them up the school drive,
more groundsmen,
longer breaks,
more sports,
more trips,
more and better furniture,
personal lockers or desks,
not having to wait outside classrooms,
provision of social areas,
teachers moving rooms rather than pupils,
more books in the library,
shorter lessons,
less homework,
more changes of teacher (not just one for a subject for two years),
more practical work.

Comments of this nature were repeated time and time again from pupils in a wide variety of schools and reflected more interest in the learning environment than in lesson content. In a similar vein the importance of relationships, particularly with the teacher, was frequently stressed. The most frequently mentioned character-istics of 'good' teachers emphasized the importance of a sense of humour, fairness and the willingness to treat pupils as individuals in their own right, creating a regime which was not too res-trictive, but one which made pupils work. It was also important that teachers should know their subject and be able to explain it clearly – whatever the subject might be.

This emphasis on what it is like to be a learner has much more in common with the attempts by the LAPP teachers to raise attainment through improving the learners' experience of school than it does with the definition of attainment targets for specific age-groups.

THE VOICE IN THE WILDERNESS

Raising attainment is a stated goal of the Education Reform Act. However, the experience of schools involved with the LAPP suggests that the identification of attainment targets is unlikely to be sufficient by itself to succeed in this goal except in the very narrowest sense. If education is only about recall of predeter-mined facts or practical activities then attainment may indeed be raised. But if education is about more than this and aims to contribute to the development of individuals with the ability to reason and possessing transferable skills, then the individual needs of learners must be considered to be at least as important as the content of the curriculum and testing.

The requirements of ERA have tended to focus attention away from the delivery and organization of education; the voice of the pupils – never a very loud voice – is in danger of being completely lost. Most people involved with education would accept that a tighter definition of the curriculum was long overdue and could greatly benefit pupils, but this should be combined with recog-nition that attainment is also related to motivation and the pupils' experience of the curriculum.

The experience of the LAPP suggests that real progress in raising attainment will only result if all the elements that go to make up education are perceived as being equally important. Content must be clearly defined and relevant to the needs both of society and of individual learners; assessment must be appropriate and reliable; last, but of equal importance, the pupils' experience of schooling must be such that they are truly motivated to learn. The ERA concentrates specifically on just two of these elements, content and assessment, the third is left to chance. Teachers involved in listening to pupils found consideration of this third element essential in any systematic reorganization of schooling. Current experience suggests that on a national basis it is unlikely that this lesson has been, or will be, learned.

REFERENCES

Clough, P and Nixon, J (1989) 'The context of change', in Clough, E, Clough, P and Nixon, J (eds) (1989) *The New Learning: Contexts and Futures for Curriculum Reform*, Basingstoke: Macmillan.

Her Majesty's Inspectorate (1989) *Education Observed 12: The Lower Attaining Pupils' Programme 1982–88*, London: Department of Education and Science.

Hughes, JM (1984) *The Best Years. Reflections of School Leavers in the 1980s*, Aberdeen: Aberdeen University Press.

Widlake, P (1985) 'How should we respond to change', in *British Journal Special Education* **12**, 1, 50–52.

Chapter 8

Teaching Thinking: Past and Present

Nigel Blagg

The task is to produce a changed environment for learning – an environment in which there is a new relationship between students and their subject matter, in which knowledge and skill become objects of interrogation, enquiry and extrapolation. As individuals acquire knowledge, they should also be empowered to think and reason. (Glaser, 1984, p. 26)

INTRODUCTION

We live in times of rapid social and technological change. In some fields new information becomes obsolete within weeks, days or even hours. Indeed, the knowledge explosion has reached the point where as Toffler (1970) implied, the future arrived yesterday. For many of us, our everyday circumstances change so frequently that we could be forgiven for feeling like Alice in Wonderland who replying to the question, 'Who are you?' confessed:

I – I hardly know, sir, at present – at least I know who I was when I got up this morning, but I think I must have changed several times since then. (Lewis Carroll, 1911)

What does this time of change mean for education? Knowledge is accumulating at such a rate that it is impossible to learn everything. Moreover, as knowledge is transitory, it is difficult to predict what will be useful for the future or what to select to learn. Therefore, we must teach children how to think and learn i.e. equip them with the basic attitudes, beliefs, skills and resources necessary to tackle fresh problems and acquire new information.

This does not imply that we should teach general thinking and problem solving skills separate to or at the expense of knowledge acquisition. Indeed, the ability to think and reason is context related and knowledge dependent. For instance, one cannot expect pupils to understand and apply the principles of classification without having 'expert' knowledge about the subject matter to be classified. Nevertheless, at the present time, many pupils perceive learning as a series of unrelated and discrete experiences. Skills and procedures with the potential for generalization become contextually welded to the circumstances in which they are learned. It is as though each task is treated as an entirely novel experience rather than one that builds on previous learning. What ought to be a continuous learning process can become an erratic and episodic experience with pupils being unable to make links between past and present learning, either within or between subject disciplines.

Teaching how to learn needs to be an integral part of the whole curriculum with both pupils and teachers appreciating interrelationships between content and process issues across subjects. Given the knowledge explosion we are facing, it does seem essential that curriculum planners should make greater efforts to select and organize what to teach so that factual and procedural knowledge acquired in one subject supports learning and development in other subjects.

Interestingly, this problem has been recognized for some years in the vocational training field where much time and energy has been spent on researching ways of training for transfer i.e. training in such a way that skills and ideas acquired in one context are readily applied to a range of new contexts. A major study by Wolf (1990) has highlighted that transfer can be enhanced by giving trainees many and varied experiences beyond their vocational area and using whole complex tasks (rather than teaching sub-skills remote from real life problems). At the same time, considerable energy has been spent on identifying and teaching core skills i.e. skills and procedural knowledge common to many different jobs and contexts. This rests on the theory that if these basic generic skills can be taught, young adults will become more flexible and adaptable learners able to acquire new skills and fresh knowledge easily as the need arises.

Recently, the Government has recognized the importance of establishing a more coherent and integrated framework for post 16 academic and vocational qualifications. In response to the Secretary of State for Education, the National Curriculum Council published a discussion document: 'Core Skills 16–19' (Graham, 1990) and a parallel report, 'Common Learning Outcomes: Core Skills in A/AS Levels and NCVQs' was published by The National Council for Vocational Qualifications (Jessup, 1990). Amongst other things, both reports strongly emphasize the importance of identifying, developing and assessing skills associated with communication, personal autonomy and problem solving.

Curiously, the National Curriculum barely addresses these issues. Indeed, it still reflects much of the compartmentalism that has existed in schools for years. The orders for the core and foundation subjects contain loose statements about selected aspects of declarative and procedural knowledge deemed essential by each of the subject working parties. Within the subjects, areas of knowledge have been grouped into attainment targets and levels of difficulty but there is no coherent integrative plan that maps relationships between content and process issues within and across the various subjects.

Of course, core skills are already addressed haphazardly in schools but it is rare to find these general transferable issues being considered as central to curriculum planning. However, there is a growing interest in a variety of intellectual and/or social skills training programmes that attempt to tackle core skills in a more systematic and comprehensive way. The Somerset Thinking Skills Couse (STSC) provides an important example of one of the many approaches currently in use throughout the UK. This chapter will review theoretical and practical issues associated with the development and application of STSC and consider the significance of the programme for schools today.

TEACHING THINKING – HISTORICAL ISSUES

You teach science; well and good; I am busy fashioning the tools for its acquisition . . . . (Rousseau, 1762, p. 90)

The idea of teaching thinking skills dates back to the time of Socrates and Plato and has been championed by philosophers and educationalists throughout the centuries. There has always been a debate about the merits of directive versus experiential learning, and rote learning versus learning through understanding. Rote learning approaches with their emphasis on instruction and direction do have the advantage of ensuring the acquisition of particular facts and routines. All too often though, such learning lacks understanding, is short term and situation specific. More experiential, facilitative approaches can create the circumstances for deeper understanding but nevertheless require more time, effort and planning to ensure that pupils acquire the intended knowledge, concepts and skills. Nowadays, most teachers recognize the importance of experiential and interactive approaches to learning and for many, Socratic dialogue has become the cornerstone of their approach. Nevertheless, sufficient attention is rarely given to the structure and organization of learning. Interactive approaches alone do not lead to better understanding.

Another common debate has centred around what should be taught and in particular, the wider benefits of teaching certain subjects. For example, educationalists have suggested that the study of subjects such as mathematics, logic or Latin can prepare pupils for other learning tasks. Indeed, during the discussion stages of the National Curriculum the Secretary of State was lobbied on these matters by various subject interest groups. The relevance of Latin has been given fresh significance by 'Lingo', a programme for schools by Spooner (1988) which explores the etymological roots of our language, thereby helping pupils to appreciate the structure and meaning of important words necessary for coping with the concepts that are fundamental to progress in learning.

At the beginning of this century, study skills were in vogue. Numerous books and manuals were published providing tips and guidance on issues such as how to pass examinations and methods of memorizing. All too often, advice was too general to be of use and in any case applied too late in the school career when habits and routines were already well established. Much of this advice lacked any theoretical or empirical basis. In spite of this, study skills are still popular, with many of the old ideas revamped, repackaged and passed on as enduring truths (Nisbet and Shucksmith, 1986).

However, serious attempts to teach pupils how to learn have been hampered by deeply entrenched views about the nature of intelligence. For many, the ability to learn has been viewed as an immodifiable expression of a fixed and inherited *quantity* of intelligence. This view has not only been popular in educational circles but also in society at large. Even before children come to school, many have been labelled by their parents as bright or slow. All too often, this labelling process continues throughout the school years and becomes a self-fulfilling prophecy.

Enduring myths about the immutability of intelligence have been perpetuated by the numerous tests that have been designed to measure this hypothetical construct. Although intelligence tests are at best indicators of previous learning they have been regarded by many as being able to indicate potential for learning. Moreover, even though numerous studies have indicated the dramatic influence of educational experience on IQs (Clarke and Clarke, 1976) outmoded notions about the invariant nature of IQs still persist.

RECENT DEVELOPMENTS – RESEARCH AND THEORY

Nevertheless, there are grounds for optimism. The limitations of IQs are now being widely recognized and new ways of assessing potential for learning are being explored through the dynamic testing movement (Lidz, 1987). The old Piagetian notion that children will learn when they are ready is now being replaced by a much more active and positive Vygotskian premise that intellectual development is an outcome of educational experience rather than a necessary prerequisite for it. Increasingly, the significance of social interaction in learning is being recognized by schools with far more emphasis being placed on work undertaken in small groups. Finally, the crucial role of language as a mediator of learning and a regulator of behaviour is highlighted in the National Oracy Project and in the Statutory Orders for the English National Curriculum 5–16.

These developments also coincide with an explosive growth in research on metacognition (an individual's conscious awareness of his own thought processes). Campione, et al. (1982) have demonstrated that young children and older low achievers are far less knowledgeable than adults or high achievers about methods of learning and problem solving. It has been suggested that the key to successful learning may depend upon helping learners to acquire a broader repertoire of cognitive strategies and gain conscious control over them. Of course this in turn depends upon being able to identify and define widely applicable (core) problem solving strategies. This is no easy matter (for a detailed discussion see Blagg, 1990).

Information processing analyses of intelligence have attempted to identify important mental processes underlying numerous intellectual tasks. This has led to many different suggestions about the nature of metacognition with each researcher using his own specialist language and terms of reference. As yet, there is no commonly agreed taxonomy of cognitive skills nor even an agreed list of essential skills. Nevertheless, as Nisbet and Shucksmith (1986) and Blagg (1990) point out, there is broad agreement in the literature on the main domains that need attention. One can distinguish between two broad groups of teachable, cognitive skills referred to in STSC as:

- cognitive resources (specific lower order skills and techniques); and
- cognitive strategies (co-ordinated sequences of skills and procedures selected for a particular purpose).

Research evidence is accumulating to suggest that both resources and strategies can be taught and there are many positive suggestions on ways of ensuring that such skills and procedures transfer to fresh learning contexts (Blagg, 1990).

THE SOMERSET LOWER ATTAINING PUPILS PROJECT (LAPP)

The Somerset LAPP which began in 1983 involved three elements:

1. A programme of residential and community enabling experiences.
2. The implementation and evaluation of an intellectual skills training programme known as Instrumental Enrichment (Feuerstein, *et al.*, 1980).
3. A series of teacher secondments exploring new ways of adapting and developing aspects of the school curriculum to help lower achieving pupils.

The project was located in Bridgwater and involved fourth and fith year pupils and their teachers from the four mainstream secondary schools in the town. Extra resources, favourable teaching ratios and scale posts were made available in each of the project schools to facilitate the development of the project. Dr Nigel Blagg was appointed as the evaluator of the Instrumental Enrichment (IE) component of LAPP and Mike Baxter co-ordinated and evaluated the other elements of the project.

The IE evaluation started at the beginning of 1984 during the second year of the project. By that stage, some of the initial teething problems associated with a rapid implementation had been ironed out and teachers were beginning to come to terms with an unfamiliar, abstract curriculum. The evaluation was extensive, involving both experimental and control groups for both pupils and teachers. Approximately 250 pupils and 30 teachers were tested pre and post on a range of cognitive, behavioural and attitudinal measures. Some of these measures involved existing standardized procedures and others were specially developed for the evaluation (Blagg, 1990). In addition, observational data were gathered throughout the two year study and anecdotal information was gathered via termly diaries kept by teachers and loosely structured interviews with each teacher and a sample of the pupils. The findings and implications of this study have been reported in Blagg (1990).

Towards the end of the first year of the IE evaluation, detailed observations of both pupils and teachers highlighted some of the benefits and drawbacks of IE. Certainly from the teachers' point of view, involvement with IE and the underlying theoretical ideas generated much careful thought and analysis about the nature of teaching and the process of learning. Many teachers began to appreciate basic deficiencies in pupils which they had previously chosen to ignore or had failed to notice. Within the IE programme, basic cognitive skills and issues were exposed, developed and practised. Many of these skills (e.g. the ability to compare and classify; analyse and synthesize; recognize and define tasks with reference to both implicit and explicit information) were seen to be fundamental across the curriculum.

Nevertheless, although pupils became conscious of these kinds of skills whilst managing abstract IE tasks there was little evidence of pupils transferring the processes to other curriculum areas. Perhaps this was not surprising given the problems teachers experienced in providing examples of suitable 'bridging' activities to help pupils apply IE skills to everyday life. In addition, other concerns about IE were beginning to surface. For example, pupils complained that some of the materials were inappropriate to their age and interests and that there was too much repetition creating boredom. In the main, IE tasks called for a serialistic, analytic approach. This was fine for impulsive children who needed to learn to be more reflective but not so good for those pupils who were already over-reflective, perfectionistic and anxious about making mistakes. Moreover, the contextually bare, 'IQ-like' appearance of the IE exercises and the heavily prescriptive nature of the programme meant that it was a fairly inflexible 'bolt-on' curriculum that was difficult to integrate with other subjects.

It was clear that even if the post-test data were to demonstrate unequivocally positive benefits to pupils and teachers, it would be unlikely that the programmes would be disseminated widely once special funding had been withdrawn. The purchase of the programme was costly; the exercises could not be photocopied so that each year, fresh materials for each pupil would need to be purchased; the abstract and very unfamiliar nature of the materials meant that lengthy training was essential and in any case, this was a condition of purchase and use i.e. it was not enough for one teacher to be trained in a school and then train and support others. Thus, it was estimated that the annual purchase costs and training implications for IE would put the programme outside the scope of most school and LEA budgets.

It was for these and many other reasons that Somerset established a curriculum team in 1985 to develop and pilot materials and training workshops for our own thinking skills course, tailored to meet mainstream secondary school needs. In the early stages of this work it was decided to create activities that would be suitable for pupils from 11 to 16 years throughout the mainstream ability range. Feedback on the materials from both experienced IE teachers and those new to cognitive skills work was very positive. It was heartening to see the kinds of teacher change issues noticeable in the early stages of IE were now being duplicated with our own materials. Pupil reaction to the programme was also very enthusiastic, especially amongst mixed ability pupils in the first three years of secondary school. So far, a handbook and six modules have been published with a further two modules in preparation.

THE SOMERSET THINKING SKILLS COURSE (STSC)

Aims and objectives

The STSC has been designed with a major goal in mind: to help pupils become more effective learners. There are a number of specific aims underlying this general aim:

1. To enhance self-esteem.
2. To promote positive attitudes and beliefs about being able to learn to learn.
3. To heighten awareness of learning styles and the need to adjust them according to differing demands.
4. To enhance ability to communicate ideas accurately and clearly.
5. To teach basic cognitive resources underpinning problem-solving processes.
6. To develop awareness and control over the use of problem-solving processes.
7. To transform passive recipients of information into active searchers and generators of ideas.
8. To facilitate the ability to transfer and generalize ideas across many different contexts. (Blagg, *et al.*, 1988a)

These specific aims relate to the core skill domains emphasized in Graham (1990) and Jessup (1990) i.e. personal autonomy, communication skills and problem-solving abilities, as Figure 8.1 illustrates.

Design issues

Many of the factors that influenced STSC design have already been alluded to, including: lessons learned from practical experience with IE; implications of recent theory and research related to teaching for transfer and various curriculum trends emphasizing interactive teaching approaches, problem solving, small group work and oracy.

These different influences persuaded us to:

- include appropriate and sufficient content in pupil activities to make STSC meaningful and relevant;
- produce teacher guidelines with enough detail to allow for distanced learning;
- use a wide range of novel, visually based discussion tasks relatively free from previous failure situations;
- emphasize small group work, enabling pupils to help one another, compare and share ideas and reflect on skills, procedures and solutions;
- include open-ended tasks allowing for various levels of interpretation, multiple solutions and differentiation by outcome;

Cognitive Demands

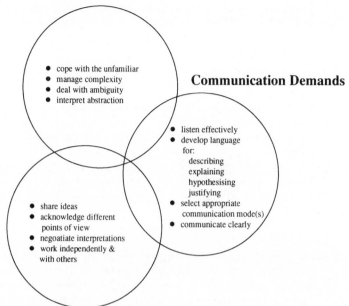

- cope with the unfamiliar
- manage complexity
- deal with ambiguity
- interpret abstraction

Communication Demands

- listen effectively
- develop language
  for:
  - describing
  - explaining
  - hypothesising
  - justifying
- select appropriate
  communication mode(s)
- communicate clearly

- share ideas
- acknowledge different
  points of view
- negoatiate interpretations
- work independently &
  with others

Personal & Social Demands

Figure 8.1 Illustrating overlapping themes underpinning STSC

- include contrasting closed tasks requiring more systematic and serialistic approaches emphasizing precision and accuracy; and
- allow for easily accessible materials, freely photocopiable within schools.

Moreover, in order to optimize the chances of transfer and generalization, we designed STSC:

- as a cross curricular, modular course allowing for integration with various curriculum areas;
- using complex, ambiguous and challenging problem-solving tasks presented in a variety of modes across different content areas; and
- so that there were clear links between skills and processes involved in the programme and their wider applications to interpersonal and curriculum areas.

Theoretical model

Self esteem. It can be seen from the foregoing that STSC is not confined to purely cognitive matters. We have also been concerned with motivational, social and communication issues (see

Blagg *et al.*, 1988b and Blagg, 1990). For example, many of the STSC tasks have been designed to promote children's confidence and self esteem. The underlying philosophy of the course emphasizes the importance of establishing a safe and democratic environment in which:

- pupils' ideas are carefully considered and valued both by other pupils and the teacher;
- misunderstandings and errors are handled sensitively and constructively;
- pupils are encouraged to challenge ideas rather than personalities;
- it is safe and acceptable to hold a different view from the majority, provided it can be justified; and
- it is good to ask questions, both of oneself and of others. (Blagg, 1990, p. 152)

Learning styles.   We have been concerned to produce materials that allow teachers to encourage the adoption of appropriate learning styles for different types of task – so many children exhibit an all-pervasive learning style, irrespective of the context or situation. For example, children with learning problems are often impulsive (Kagan, *et al.*, 1964) tending to answer questions before they know what the problem is or rush through tasks without paying sufficient attention to planning, accuracy or detail. Thus, we have designed a number of relatively closed, serialistic tasks that do demand systematic work and painstaking attention to detail. At the other end of the continuum there are some children who fail at school because they are over-reflective, constantly checking and rechecking information or plans without ever committing themselves to paper. These children often seem unable to take risks, make guesses or make a rapid holistic appraisal of a problem. Typically, they work very slowly and incredibly neatly, being unable to produce a quick and rough version of a piece of work. Many of our open–ended stimulus tasks provide opportunities for helping pupils with this kind of difficulty as these tasks involve generating and testing multiple hypotheses about conflicting evidence.

The intellectual level

At an intellectual level, we have been concerned to promote the acquisition, application and generalization of both purposeful cognitive strategies and the underlying cognitive resources on which they are based (see Figure 8.2).

The distinction between cognitive resources and cognitive strategies has been helpfully clarified by Nisbet and Shucksmith (1986) who draw a simple analogy between a football team and its

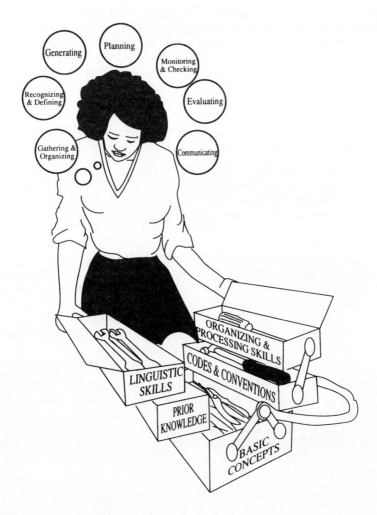

Figure 8.2 Illustration of the thinker's need for a range of cognitive resources to build purposeful strategies (taken from Blagg, 1990)

trainer. Individual players need to be fluent with many different skills such as dribbling, heading, accurate passing and so on. Nevertheless, skills are not enough. Skills need to be purposefully sequenced into tactics or strategies. However, possession of skills and tactics would not ensure success. Above all, the team needs to be able to monitor and adapt its strategies to suit the particular circumstances on the field, i.e. flexibility is required. The same kind of reasoning applies to pupils in school. The acquisition of skills and tactics might be fine for coping with very particular circumstances but would not ensure that pupils were competent in coping with less familiar tasks or problems. Pupils need to acquire the higher level control procedures that govern the selection, co-ordination and sequencing of skills and strategies. Metacognitivists like Flavell (1977) and Campione *et al.* (1982) argue that if pupils can become more conscious of their own thought processes when solving problems they may in turn gain better control over these processes.

Cognitive strategies.   At a strategic level, we have chosen to focus on a number of domains, typically associated with problem solving:

- gathering and organizing (information);
- recognizing (a problem exists);
- defining (the problem);
- generating (alternative approaches);
- planning (mentally testing and selecting the most viable approach);
- checking (self monitoring);
- evaluating (testing solutions and approaches);
- communicating (the outcomes to self and others);
- transferring and generalizing (actively reflecting on the application of skills and procedures learned in one context to many others – deducing principles or rules to assist future learning or problem solving).

For the purposes of STSC, we have subsumed these domains within our own problem-solving loop. Figure 8.3. illustrates examples of strategic issues involved in each domain. Whilst the diagram implies a natural sequence, numbers and directional arrows have been omitted in recognition of the fact that real life problem solving is rarely a straightforward uni-directional sequence. For instance, we may often reach the planning stage and then need to return to data gathering before continuing. At the monitoring stage, we may discover that our working procedures are quite inappropriate and need a radical revision.

Cognitive resources.   Within STSC, cognitive resources are mainly concerned with:

- organizing and processing skills;
- knowledge and experience of codes and conventions; and
- linguistic skills.

Organizing and processing skills (e.g. scanning and focusing, analysing and synthesizing; describing and comparing; grouping and classifying and so on) are overlapping and often complementary processes that enable the child to organize, reorganize, memorize and retrieve information. Of course, each of these organizing and processing skills involves many elements which

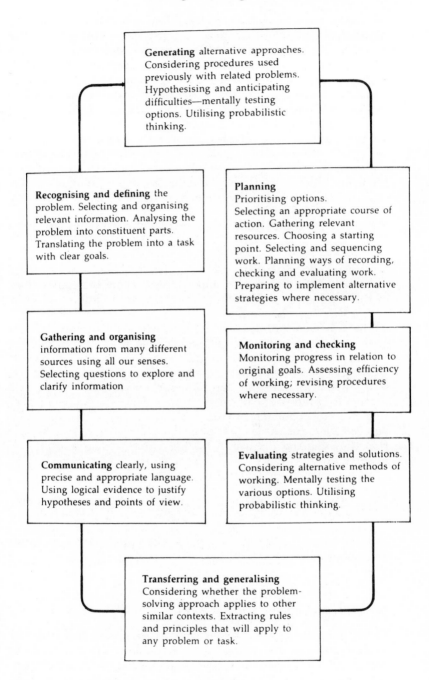

Figure 8.3 Illustration of the STSC problem-solving loop

are exposed and integrated in the STSC modules. For example, the ability to recall past experiences to solve a current problem depends in part upon being able to compare what is similar in the current situation with what has been experienced previously. It may also depend upon being able to organize and categorize events and experiences. These issues are explored in detail in Module 3, Comparative Thinking. Of course, sometimes pupils need to work at a more abstract and sophisticated level. For example, in solving a complex problem, they may need to refer back to a different but analogous situation from which they can extract principles that would be helpful with the current problem. Module 5, Understanding Analogies, unpacks many of the issues involved in understanding and using analogical thinking.

Beyond these important skills, pupils also need to understand a whole range of representational forms (both visual and verbal) e.g. abbreviations, codes, symbols, conventions and reference systems used in cartoons, pictures, charts, tables, graphs, maps and so on. They also need to appreciate concepts and conventions in time and space to allow for reflection, anticipation, ordering, prioritizing and planning.

The importance of appropriate linguistic skills cannot be over-estimated. At a very simple level, pupils need to possess the technical vocabulary to distinguish between objects and events and describe aspects of their experience accurately and clearly. Yet so often, low attainers are denied important vocabulary because it is regarded as too difficult for them to understand. All pupils need to gain a full command of language in its many forms, functions and varieties. For these reasons we have designed STSC tasks so that they demand the use of high level oracy skills and provide opportunities to address the oral areas specified by the English National Curriculum Committee:

> . . . to persuade: to explain; to instruct; to entertain; to narrate; to speculate; to argue a case; to report; to describe; to find out; to clarify or explore an issue; to solve a problem; to interpret; to summarize; to evaluate; to reflect; to announce; to criticize and respond to criticism. (*English for Ages 5-16*, DES (1989) para. 15.17)

Structure and organization of STSC

STSC involves a series of visually based tasks organized into modular themes and arranged as a spiralling linear model. As Figure 8.4 shows, the entire course involves eight modules. The first four modules are concerned with helping pupils to make connections between disparate aspects of their experience in the 'here and now'. Modules 5 and 6 help pupils to make predictions

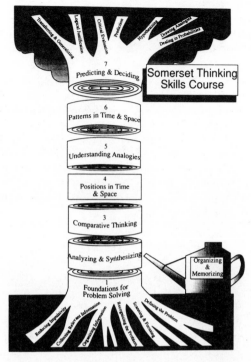

Figure 8.4 Illustration of the modular structure of the Somerset Thinking Skills Course (from the forthcoming revised edition of the STSC Handbook, Blagg, Ballinger and Gardner, in preparation c)

and go beyond their present circumstances by appreciating many of the subtle patterns and relationships that pervade our everyday lives. Module 7 is a summative module that applies the skills, strategies and principles established throughout the course to complex, everyday problems. Module 8 (Organizing and Memorizing) is intended as a supplementary unit that can be used at any stage during the course.

Within the eight modules, each pupil activity is intended to focus on particular learning style and resource issues. However, beyond this each pupil task is in itself a problem-solving activity which requires that pupils register a problem exists, carefully define it for themselves, generate and test their own plans and so on. The teacher's role is that of sensitive mediator, providing minimal prompts as necessary in order to ensure that pupils maintain maximum responsibility for dealing with each task.

In tune with the literature on teaching for transfer, each module contains a range of problem-solving tasks presented in different modes and styles and drawn from various content areas. The STSC activities can be divided into three overlapping task types:

- stimulus activities;
- artificial tasks; and
- naturalistic tasks.

Stimulus activities are small group discussion tasks which establish a meaningful context and theme as a backcloth to the rest of the activities in each module. They broaden pupil learning by offering numerous opportunities to explore connections and associations between different areas of experience. These tasks are quite complex and involve open-ended activities that foster and encourage imaginative and divergent interpretations which need to be justified by reference to the information provided. Figure 8.5 provides an example of a stimulus task taken from Module 1 (Foundations for Problem Solving).

Artificial tasks are contextually restricted activities that expose, teach and practise particular cognitive resources. Some of the tasks are 'closed' and require a very focused serialistic approach to find one particular solution, whereas others are more 'open-ended' and ambiguous with many alternative interpretations and solutions. Figure 8.6 provides an example of a relatively closed artificial task taken from the fourth module, Positions in Time and Space.

Naturalistic tasks involve problem-solving activities that relate to everyday life, enabling teachers to check for literal and figural transfer of resources exposed and practised on the artificial and stimulus tasks. Naturalistic tasks provide opportunities for the teacher to identify and assist those:

- pupils who demonstrate a knowledge of numerous cognitive resources but remain unable to select and deploy them in appropriate problem-solving contexts;
- pupils who experience strategic difficulties because they still have major gaps in their cognitive resources.

An example of a naturalistic task is given in Figure 8.7.

The eight modules can be summarized as follows:

1. *Foundations for Problem Solving* (Blagg *et al.*, 1988a) – represents the course in 'miniature' and establishes the aims, format and conventions for STSC. It includes activities that touch upon many of the resource and strategic issues elaborated on in later parts of the course. The module concentrates especially on the early stages of problem solving i.e. procedures and skills essential to gathering and organizing relevant information and recognizing and defining problems. For instance, pupils learn to scan and focus; distinguish between explicit and implicit information; use

Figure 8.5 Illustration of the 'The Living Room' – a stimulus task from STSC Module 1, Foundations for Problem Solving

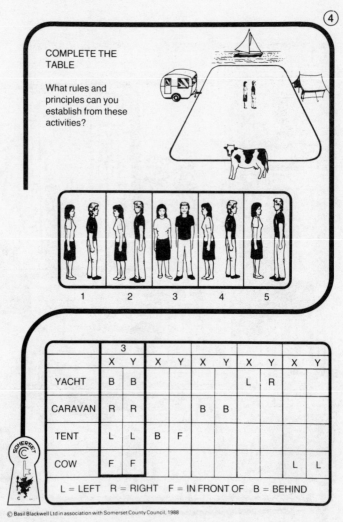

	3									
	X	Y	X	Y	X	Y	X	Y	X	Y
YACHT	B	B					L	R		
CARAVAN	R	R			B	B				
TENT	L	L	B	F						
COW	F	F							L	L

L = LEFT   R = RIGHT   F = IN FRONT OF   B = BEHIND

COMPLETE THE TABLE

What rules and principles can you establish from these activities?

Figure 8.6 Illustration of 'Orientation C', the third task in a sequence of three taken from the early part of STSC Module 4, Positions in Time and Space

systematic search strategies; describe and label essential features.

2. *Analysing and Synthesizing* (Blagg *et al.*, 1988b) – focuses more specifically on the nature of analysis and synthesis in everyday life. Pupil activities consider part–whole relationships in both structures and operations and link understanding in this area to different forms of instructions, error analysis and design issues. The final stages of the module lead on to an appreciation of the interrelationships between

Compare the items in each row and choose the most economic buys. Justify and illustrate your choices.

Figure 8.7 'Bargain Offers' taken from STSC Module 3, Comparative Thinking

structure, function and aesthetics, finishing on a complex mastery task in which pupils apply their numerous analytic skills to an evaluative exercise related to the humanities.

3. *Comparative Thinking* (Blagg *et al.*, 1988c) – distinguishes between describing and comparing before developing the nature, meaning and purpose of comparison. It explores the importance of comparative behaviour in all kinds of decision making (e.g. selecting the most economic buys in a supermarket, choosing a holiday within various constraints, etc.). The later stages of the module demonstrate how comparison forms the basis of classification before going on to explore the nature and purpose of classification in everyday life.

4. *Positions in Time and Space* (Blagg, *et al.*, 1988d) – heightens pupil awareness of temporal and spatial considerations at the heart of planning and anticipating. The module exposes and integrates key concepts and vocabulary relating to reference points in time and space. Analytic behaviour is now enhanced with specific spatial labelling systems and given a past–present future dimension. The later stages of the module broaden the activities beyond physical issues into 'mental' issues. In particular, the module considers how different people come to adopt very different 'mental positions' or viewpoints. This involves exploring the nature of empathy and prejudice.

5. *Understanding Analogies* (Blagg, *et al.*, 1989) – explores the nature of symbolism and analogy in everyday life. The module considers comparative principles involved in understanding many transformations and relationships (pictorial, figural and cartoon). The module shows how transformations can form the basis of understanding different kinds of analogies and how analogy, metaphor and simile are related.

6. *Patterns in Time and Space*, (Blagg *et al.*, 1990) – builds on Modules 4 and 5 (Positions in Time and Space and Understanding Analogies). It explores the kinds of predictions one can make from understanding temporal and spatial patterns and analogies. It includes tasks that involve an appreciation of: the relationships between time, distance and speed; complex planning and time management.

7. *Predicting and Deciding* (Blagg *et al.*, in preparation a) – integrates and summarizes aspects from previous modules in the context of a wide range of social, domestic and academic decision-making activities. It highlights the fact that most decision making is based on probabilities rather than certainties. It encourages pupils to consider how different kinds of evidence and information contribute to probabilistic thinking.

8. *Organising and Memorising* (Blagg *et al.*, in preparation b) – links with many of the ideas and resources emphasized through-

out the course, with an explicit focus on techniques and strategies to facilitate recalling, organizing and memorizing different types of information. The module (supplementary to the rest of STSC) emphasizes flexible strategic thinking through tasks that prompt pupils to consider which types of organizing and memorizing techniques and resources should be used for different purposes.

Concluding Comments

In many ways STSC was published ahead of its time. The early modules pre-date the National Curriculum and the recent debate about the need for accreditation of core skills in both academic and vocational qualifications. Many of the issues now being rehearsed in documents published by the National Curriculum Council and the National Council for Vocational Qualifications have already been explored intimately within STSC. Indeed, we have received feedback from many schools throughout the UK who are now creatively using STSC as a means of providing coherence to the National Curriculum, helping pupils to see common process links between the core and foundation subjects.

In a number of schools, STSC has made a profound impact on the whole curriculum. For example, in St Mary's School (Newcastle-upon-Tyne), all pupils now participate in the Somerset Thinking Skills Course. The six modules published so far are infused throughout the curriculum and taught in a planned sequence by different subject specialists. Moreover, the interactive and metacognitive messages involved in STSC have led to the adoption of many additional, exciting initiatives in science, mathematics, English and the humanities. Early, in-house evaluations of this approach point to exciting benefits to both pupils and teachers.

Delivery of the National Curriculum requires teachers to be confident with interactive teaching styles and able both to assess and sensitively facilitate children's development across many different areas of learning. User testimonials from schools suggest that STSC has made a contribution here as the following quotes indicate:

> STSC is for us primarily a diagnostic tool that has highlighted problems that we should have been aware of ten years ago. . . .

> The course (STSC) has helped to move staff away from their chalk and talk approach.

> I never realized how important is was to ask the right questions. Sometimes I kick myself because I know I've lost the pupils for ten minutes by asking the wrong question.

We know of many studies exploring the effects of STSC on both pupils and teachers. A study by Lake (1988) compared the effects of using Lipman's Philosophy for Children Programme with the first STSC module given under two conditions to mixed ability 10–12 year olds. The pupils (from one class) were randomly assigned to three groups and independently assessed at the beginning of the study and three months later on a factor analysed classroom observation scale (known as the GHOST scale). In one group, STSC was used to develop pupil knowledge of problem-solving processes with an emphasis on discussion, oracy and small group work. The second STSC group used the materials as independent problem-solving tasks with relatively little mediation, discussion and reflection. The third group received Lipman's programme. Put simply, the Lipman group showed a significant improvement in competence with routine classroom tasks whereas the discussion-oriented STSC group showed a significant improvement on the ability to deal with complex tasks and the management of their own learning. The STSC group that worked independently and received no mediation did not show any significant changes.

Recently, Ballinger (in preparation) completed a replication of one aspect of Blagg's (1990) IE evaluation, exploring the effects of STSC on teacher attitudinal change in two secondary schools. In common with IE, STSC was found to have a profound and positive impact on teacher attitudes both towards themselves as teachers and towards the potential of low achieving adolescents.

Teachers involved in STSC look beyond their own subject disciplines and become more conscious of promoting pupil understanding of links between different aspects of their schooling experience. Many STSC teachers begin to take on responsibility for developing intellectual skills in pupils as well as fostering academic achievement. Those that take this responsibility seriously now recognize that many pupils who appear 'less able' can be helped to go well beyond projected academic expectations.

REFERENCES

Ballinger, MP (in preparation) Unpublished M Phil Thesis – Teacher change in the Somerset Thinking Skills Course.

Blagg, NR (1990) *Can We Teach Intelligence – A Comprehensive Evaluation of Feuerstein's Instrumental Enrichment Programme*, Hove, Sussex: Lawrence Erlbaum Associates.

Blagg, NR and Ballinger, MP (1990) *Thinking to Learn, Learning to Think*, London: Routledge.

Blagg, NR, Ballinger, MP, Gardner, RJ, Petty, M and Williams, G (1988a) *Foundations for Problem Solving*, Oxford: Blackwell Education.

Blagg, NR, Ballinger, MP, Gardner, RJ, Petty, M and Williams, G (1988b) *Analysing and Synthesising*, Oxford: Blackwell Education.

Blagg, NR, Ballinger, MP, Gardner, RJ and Petty, M (1988c) *Comparative Thinking*, Oxford: Blackwell Education.

Blagg, NR, Ballinger, MP, Gardner, RJ and Petty, M (1988d) *Positions in Time and Space*, Oxford: Blackwell Education.

Blagg, NR, Ballinger, MP, and Gardner, RJ (1989) *Understanding Analogies*, Oxford: Blackwell Education.

Blagg, NR, Ballinger, MP and Gardner, RJ (1990) *Patterns in Time and Space*, Oxford: Blackwell Education.

Blagg, NR, Ballinger, MP and Gardner, RJ (in preparation a) *Predicting and Deciding*.

Blagg, NR, Ballinger, MP, and Gardner, RJ (in preparation b) *Organising and Memorising*.

Blagg, NR, Ballinger, MP, and Gardner, RJ (in preparation c) *STSC Handbook*, revised edn, Oxford: Blackwell Education.

Campione, JC, Brown, AL and Ferrara, RA (1982) 'Mental retardation and intelligence', in Sternberg RJ (ed.) *Handbook of Human Intelligence*, Cambridge: Cambridge University Press.

Carroll, L, (1911) *Alice in Wonderland*, London: William Heinemann Ltd.

Clarke, ADB, and Clarke, AM (1976) *Early Experience: Myth and evidence*, New York: Free Press.

DES (1989) *English for Ages 5–16*, London: HMSO.

Feuerstein, R, Rand, Y, Hoffman, M and Miller, R (1980) *Instrumental Enrichment*, Baltimore, MD: University Park Press.

Flavell, JH (1977) *Cognitive Development*, Englewood Cliffs, NJ: Prentice-Hall.

Glaser, R (1984) 'Education and thinking. The role of knowledge', *American Psychologist*.

Graham, DG (1990) Core Skills 16–19 – A Response to the Secretary of State, The National Curriculum Council.

Jessup, G, (1990) Common Learning Outcomes: Core Skills in A/AS Levels and NVQs, *NCVQ R&D Report No 6*.

Kagan, J, Rosman, BB, Day, D, Albert, J and Phillips, W (1964) 'Information processing in the child: Significance of analytic and reflective attitudes', *Psychological Monographs*, 78 (Whole No, 578).

Lake, M (1988) 'Group participation compared with individual problem solving', *Thinking Skills Network Newsletter*, Number 5 Issue. Milton Keynes.

Lidz, CS (ed) (1987) *Dynamic Assessment. An inter-actional approach to evaluating learning potential*, New York: Guilford Press.

Nisbet, J and Shucksmith, J (1986) *Learning Strategies*, London: Routledge and Kegan Paul.

Rousseau, JJ (1762) *Emile*, London: Everyman Edition.

Spooner, A (1988) *Lingo: A course on words and how to use them*, Bristol: Classical Press.

Toffler, A (1970) *Future Shock*, New York: Random House.

Wolf, A (1990) 'What should "teaching for transfer" mean?' Paper delivered to an invitational seminar on transfer, Warwick University, Warwick.

Chapter 9

Using 'Somerset Thinking Skills' to Promote Oracy in the Classroom

David Bowdler, Terri Webb and Stuart Dyke

INTRODUCTION

Schools are places that, *ipso facto*, value oracy and cirtical thinking. Is this the case? Children have a natural disposition to learn, but require schools to assist them with the development of a language to explain, share and criticize ideas; so necessary to sustain any challenging enquiry or problem solving. Do schools teach this language and give value to argumentative discourse and critical thinking within actual classroom activities? Can children be taught to think critically, not incidently as part of opportunities within specific subjects, but through planned provision that values speaking, listening and reasoning?

To provide a classroom response for some of these questions, a research project was completed in a Service Children's Middle School in Germany. As part of the school's contribution to the National Oracy Project a class of 9–10 year olds of mixed ability experienced the introduction of the Somerset Thinking Skills Modules into their curriculum. An evaluation of this Project follows a short outline of some of the assumptions on which the classroom work was established.

ORACY IN THE CLASSROOM

With the advent of the National Curriculum there is a necessity to promote children's abilities in both speaking and listening. To do this one needs to review present classroom practice and identify those language areas that in general are not being adequately developed.

The approach to oracy in classrooms has been a little haphazard, relying mainly on developing resticted modes of discourse, such as the experimental mode (anecdotal), the operational mode (stating rules and expectations) and the expositional mode (stating information).

Reports from the Assessment of Performance Unit (APU) suggest that there is a need to use different kinds of language in describing, instructing, analysing, hypothesizing, evaluating and justifying. There is evidence that pupils have no problems in describing, narrating and instructing, but have great difficulty with the higher-order language skills (Blagg et al., 1988). The development of these higher-order language skills, vital to the establishment of effective cognitive resources, are the hypothetical mode (tentative specula-tion) and the argumentative mode (challenging other viewpoints). To enable these language skills to appear, effective discussion needs to facilitate and generate ideas and establish interaction. But what constitutes effective discussion? There are the all too familiar scenarios of the teacher talking too much and of teacher directed discussion with the use of closed questioning. This results in pupils being so concerned with providing the 'right' answer, that they do not develop appropriate problem-solving strategies. In a bid to avoid this, teachers may develop open-ended discussions in which they play a minimum part in directing; however it is debatable as to whether this leads to pupils listening to one another, or to their reaching any conclusions.

As a blend of the above approaches, guided discussion is probably the most effective approach. The teacher as facilitator guides the discussion with objectives in mind, following through pupils' contributions, developing unusual responses as well as refocusing the group on the main purpose of the activity. This is particularly important where the class discusses as a whole, and in small groups, and then reconvenes.

In order for pupils to develop independent thinking and become more responsible for their own learning, pupils should be encour-aged to initiate questions. This in turn leads to pupils challenging one another's ideas and perhaps those of the teacher. Pupils are then forced to justify their own reasoning and hypotheses. It is also important to allow preperatory thinking time and encourage the pupils to understand its value for the later discussion.

Many pupils may possess the ability to perform well in the language arts but for some reason have never displayed it (Wilkinson, 1971). Thus the question arises of how the teacher can provide a context for extending speaking and listening skills. Although various educationists have described classroom activi-ties and materials that meet this difficulty, at least in part (Tann, 1990), it was decided to look at the materials of the Somerset Thinking Skills Course (Blagg et al, 1988) as a basis for a more systematic and structured approach to the development of critical thinking.

As Blagg and colleagues summarize: 'The Somerset Thinking Skills course consists of a series of modules designed to teach, discuss and generalize specific concepts, skills and strategies involved in problem solving'. (The two modules available at the time were Module 1, Foundations for Problem Solving and Module 2 Analysing and Synthesizing).

The authors stress that it is not enough to merely expose pupils to different problem-solving situations, as this alone will not allow the transfer of skills to fresh contexts. The crux of the STS approach is that of the teacher as mediator. Through effective mediation the pupils will be able to transfer learnt skills to other subject areas and to everyday life.

Recent curricular developments, such as TVEI, LAPP, GCSE, and the National Curriculum, stress the need for pupils to become more efficient with regard to problem-solving processes. The emphasis is now, more than ever, on developing pupils' abilities to organize their own learning. It is not enough, however, to assume that with new curriculum innovations pupils will magically *learn to learn*. Blagg *et al.* (1988) suggest that there is much evidence to show that this just does not happen. They believe that individuals can be trained in thinking skills, thereby improving their ability to learn.

The Somerset Thinking Skills programme is about developing flexible thinkers. Children need to be prepared to handle unfamiliar problems and learning tasks independently. In order to be able to do this they need to be able to transfer and apply (generalize) skills, strategies and procedures, learnt in particular situations, to new contexts. If they can understand the problem-solving processes involved in tasks, then they may be able to select these processes for use with similar tasks.

Approaches to learning are closely related to attitudes, beliefs and motivation. Many children often omit an important stage in organizing their learning – the planning stage. Children need to be specifically taught to plan.

Previous learning experiences do have a bearing on a child's approach to learning tasks. When children lose self-confidence and develop a poor self-image through constant criticism or they experience failure on a continuous basis, they may learn to never expect success. Similarly, a child who has never been encouraged to work independently may acquire 'learned helplessness' and be dependent on the teacher for help. Over-simplification of learning tasks can lead to children being insufficiently challenged and therefore lacking the motivation to succeed; this in turn may encourage low-expectations of the child by the teacher (Rosenthal and Jacobson, 1968).

Another attribute of the under achieving child is impulsiveness. Guesswork becomes the principal approach to learning situations, with insufficient time and thought being given to defining the task and gathering and organizing information. The STS programme enables the teacher as mediator to encourage the pupil to reflect, before selecting a particular strategy. This is important as most children use preferred styles of working, irrespective of the problem or context. The rationale behind the STS is that of helping the pupil to realize that problem solving requires the selection and application of different strategies and that these can be learned. Confidence leads to competence. This is of particular benefit to the less confident child who has adopted the 'play safe' strategy, rather than risk the possibility of failure.

The STS programme offers a wide range of activities which serve as a springboard for each lesson. The pupils are constantly required to recognize and define different types of tasks and generate, monitor and evaluate different methods of working. This wide variation enables the teacher to develop and assess the transfer of skills and strategies across the curriculum.

Some of the STS tasks are open-ended and others require more specific answers. Both approaches require the child to justify their interpretations and to evaluate and communicate clearly their solutions and methods of working. Both types of task contain an element of ambiguity, for which there are various reasons as outlined by Blagg *et al.* (1988):

a) pupils are required to think for themselves in defining the tasks;

b) use of ambiguity encourages many justifiable interpretations, prompting much debate and discussion;

c) the range of possible interpretations encourages close attention to detail;

d) it reduces impulsivity by communicating to pupils that none of the tasks is straightforward and have to be thought through;

e) in the knowledge that the teacher is not looking for set answers, the more reticent child is more likely to contribute to class discussion;

f) pupils are made more aware of the need for precision and accuracy in many everyday communications to avoid confusion and unintentional ambiguity; and

g) it encourages pupils to search for implicit and explicit clues, and for what is not implied as well as analysing the obvious details. This is an important aspect of successful academic performance.

A brief explanation now follows as to how the research project was organized based on these assumptions.

THE ORACY/STS CLASS

An agreement was made with the Headteacher to run the STS programme under the aegis of the National Oracy Project. The course was run as part of the curriculum in one mainstream class of mixed ability 9 – 10 year old children. It was discussed with the children and parents and commenced in January 1989; the following is an account of the classroom practice.

To enable children to engage openly in discussion of the STS instruments, consideration needed to be given to the physical seating arrangements. Children needed to see, and be seen by others to ensure that the full message (verbal and non-verbal) was being received. After experimenting with different classroom layouts, the most manageable structure was found to be with the tables and chairs arranged in a horseshoe shape, to maximize eye contact, to distribute opportunities equally, and to avoid leadership status. The class agreed on this arrangement. Within the horseshoe shape they were able to organize themselves for independent, paired and small group working, as well as coming together for whole class discussion.

Before starting the discussion, the children accepted that certain rules must be established, in order to avoid the outbreak of a chaotic free-for-all. Together the following rules were agreed:

- only one person spoke at a time.
- everyone listened whilst one person was speaking.
- all contributions were valued.
- people must speak clearly.
- people can challenge statements, but not the person.
- if people are called on to contribute but need more thinking time, then the slogan 'just a minute, let me think' should be adopted.
- people must try to avoid hands up, to discourage impulsivity.
- people are invited to speak or wait for a gap.
- when working in small groups one person should be elected as scribe and one as spokesperson.
- groups should consist of boys and girls.

These rules, hopefully, allowed language to proceed and operate in a way which sustained the discussion. The children understood that these rules were a tool to discussion and not an end in themselves.

The introduction to the lesson was important for establishing interest in the key concept to be taught. The introduction normally drew on children's own experiences and most children could be encouraged to contribute. It was vital either at the end of the introduction, or when the task had been introduced, that the teacher asked the children if they could see the connection. In order to achieve effective mediation the child needed to understand that the teacher had an intention to communicate something, and that this interaction must involve feedback from the child (reciprocity). Second, the meaning and purpose of the interaction must be fully clear to the child (Feuerstein *et al.*, 1979).

After a few lessons the class was able to anticipate what the lesson was going to be about.

Although the children were grouped for work each child was given a task sheet and asked to 'scan it for the main features'. At this stage some started discussing and others perused in silence. After a couple of minutes each child was expected to make a contribution as to what they thought the task was all about. The more reserved child would be asked to contribute first, before the more obvious ideas had been noted by the other children. At the beginning of the course, the class listened to each individual's contribution, and when a particularly interesting point was raised it would be opened for discussion. Once the pupils became more confident about talking, they changed the rules. Individual comments were immediately challenged and the contributor was very quickly forced to justify his thinking. The children found this stage of the lesson stimulating. As one girl commented: 'I really like Thinking Skills, it makes me feel like a politician, and I like the feeling of everyone listening to you'. Another child stated amusingly: 'I have so many ideas to think about I feel my brain is going to burst because it get so hot'.

The class discussion was followed by individual or group work. The class was tasked with a particular question or questions, and given about ten minutes for the activity. During this time the role of the teacher was to mediate, making sure each child understood the intention of the task. An example of a typical contribution follows:

> I think it's all about explicit rules. 1066 is a piece of history which is always going to be there like the Second World War. The map is an explicit rule because its always there and you've got certain rules on how to use it. The timetable, well, you have to follow it so thats an explicit rule. I'm not sure about the sign post and the Indian lady, except that the sign post tells you which way to go. The hills, well there's sayings like as old as the hills and they're things that are always there, so they're really strong rules. You see the pyramids have been there for hundreds of years and no one has ever broken them down. They can never be moved because they are just a piece of history that is so important.

Each group had a scribe and spokesperson, organized on a rotation basis, who reported back on their hypotheses. The class commented on their findings and together summarized what had been learned. This final stage of the lesson enabled the class to understand that the skills and resources which they had learned could be directly transferred to other curriculum areas and real life situations.

The bridging, or transfer, of thinking skills was integral to the teaching style of STS. An example of this was in 'planning'. This involved children simplifying complex tasks into manageable chunks. They could then reassemble the tasks and develop meaningful solutions to the problems posed. The transfer was primarily pursued in English, Art, Science and Technology where the children were encouraged to transfer the skills into the subject areas. This enabled the children to possess, as part of their intellectual armoury, a critical awareness of their own planning skills and to use them in a dynamic and appropriate way.

ASSESSMENT PROCEDURES

A variety of formal and informal assessment procedures were used. These were as follows:

Formal procedures

a) *Bristol Social Adjustment Guides*
These Guides can be described as a halfway house between ratings and more detailed short-term behaviour observations. The teacher has to underline the descriptions of behaviour which best suit the child.
Method: The CDT teacher of the class completed the 'Child in School Guide' (on all children) at the beginning of the year, 1989, and at its academic close, summer 1989.
b) *British Ability Scales (BAS) : Verbal Fluency*
This test requires children to give as many disparate/creative ideas as they can about picture cues and improbable situations.
Method: A local psychologist completed the scale on children at the beginning of the academic year, unfortunately that person left and another psychologist completed the re-test. (It was felt that because of this disparity in assessment only a general observation should be made).
c) *Cognitive Instrument for Assessing Developmental Features of Oral Argument*
This instrument is currently being piloted in a variety of Service Children's Schools. It was decided to use the instrument in preference to the National Curriculum statements of attainment for Speaking and Listening, as the latter were felt to be too broad and lacking any clear cognitive developmental features.
Five significant areas of development are highlighted by the instrument:

1) Outline of ideas.
2) Clarifying of ideas.
3) Supporting with evidence.
4) Knowledge about argumentative language.

5) Appreciation of ideas.

Method: A tape recorder was used to record the dialogue and the response partner approach utilized to gain agreement on the interpretations to be placed on each individual contribution.

Informal procedures

a) *Attitude questionnaire*
A semantic differential, five point rating scale was devised by the authors to gauge whether the children believed there had been a shift in their approaches:

- to life – 'How do you feel about your appearance? – tidy/ untidy'
- to work – 'How good do you feel you are at Maths? – very good/poor'

Method: The STS/Oracy children and a class group of similar age children (control group) completed this at the start of the year, 1989, and at its academic close, Summer 1989.
b) *Children's remarks*
Method: Other teachers asked the children about Somerset Thinking Skills and about the transfer of the skills to other lessons and to real life situations.
c) *Other teachers' remarks*
Method: Other teachers reported back on children's approach to tasks in their lessons.
d) *Observation of STS lessons by other teachers*
Method: A number of teachers, on an individual basis, sat in on the lessons as observers.

RESULTS

It is important in terms of the analysis of the results to be aware that often a school which serves a service community suffers greatly from 'turbulence' (constant movement). Many children in the class had been in eight different schools by the age of 9 years. This turbulence directly affected a) the attitude questionnaire results as only 15 of the STS class and 13 of the control class remained; and b) the BSAG results, which were completed in the last few days of term, when only 11 of the children were available.

Formal procedures

a) *Attitude questionnaire*
Of the 18 items assessed there were four which showed a highly

positive shift in favour of the STS class over the 'control' class. They were:

'How well do you tell people about things?'
- many of the children felt that they had improved in explaining their thoughts to others (a shift of +10 points over the control group).

'When you come to a piece of work, do you like to rush into it or take your time?'
- many children felt that they had become less impulsive (a shift of +6 points over the control group).

'How do you find sitting still and getting on with your work?'
- most children believed that their attention time and concentration on task had improved (a shift of +10 points over the control group).

'When the class are discussing do you like to put your hand up and tell them your ideas?'
- all children felt more confident and assertive in this situation (a shift of +25 points over the control group).

b) *British Social Adjustment Guide*
In social adjustment the gains were mainly in:

- facing new learning tasks where half of the children were now regarded as 'liking the challenge of something difficult' (previously none);
- possessing better strategies for looking after their belongings, all (as opposed to 6 previously);
- 'asking teacher's help' - eight children seek help only when necessary (as opposed to three previously);
- 'answering questions' - five, (as opposed to one), were now always ready to answer; and
- 'ways with other children' - now seven are generally kind and helpful to other children in the work situation.

c) *BAS: Verbal Fluency*
The results indicated that all the children gained in verbal fluency on the six measures employed.

d) *Cognitive Instrument/Oral Argument*
The results indicated that the pupils' use of speculative thinking and argumentative terms has increased. These higher order language skills have developed alongside their ability to recognize another's viewpont and their ability to evaluate other contributions, by offering alternative hypotheses. Finally they have shown an ability to appreciate and understand the importance of using evidence to support a hypothesis and develop an argument.

The use of the Cognitive Instrument has enabled analysis of the criteria in a very detailed way, creating an awareness of the increase in sophistication of the different levels of argument. It has also helped to reflect the development of interaction between the children, with particular emphasis on evaluating a contribution by offering an alternative hypothesis and by building on the contributions of others. This particular language style, or behaviour, is vital for effective discussion and argument.

It was felt that the children developed the ability for sustained discussion, listening to different viewpoints and were able to modify their own hypotheses, in the light of other opinions.

There follow, below, some edited examples of five children responding to a picture from Module 2 of STS. The teacher's intervention was non-judgemental and minimal. (Initially, the outcomes remain in the area of introductory outlining of ideas and limited explanation. But the teacher's efforts begin to pay dividends, as she prompts Sarah to offer more).

Teacher: Is there any more, anything else?

Sarah: It looks like the skeleton is watching the lady, and maybe the man who's speaking to the other man. . . maybe they're saying that they've seen the face, or they've had a fire, or something like that. And the lady who's looking through the magnifying glass, she could be looking at something like sugar? And the man, who's just put up the shelves, wants to see if they're wobbly and if they're steady enough to stay . . . and if you can put stuff and they won't fall down. And the lady is checking the car, so that it won't break down in the middle of the motorway.

(3b and 4b: In this introductory outlining of ideas, one of the pupils begins to 'shift cognitive gear' and offers some interpretative evidence to support her assertions).

Alison: They've all got something in common. On the police station one, the man in the chair, who is being questioned about something, he's thinking about the answer. And on the laboratory one, she's thinking about what it looks like. And down on the third one, she's thinking about how to space out the water. And on the fourth one, she's thinking where to put it.

(3d: Alison is starting to use pictorial evidence to construct a form of basic hypothesis).

Teacher: Yes, that's a very good point.

Stuart: The thing is, where you, how you, put them . . . the pieces of the jigsaw . . . into that part where it fits in.

(2b: Further clarifying of ideas, without challenge to others).

Alison: You've got to think where to put it in.

(2d: Alison is now very engaged and appears to challenge others in her manner of contribution.)

Ben: It might not be part of that part.

(2c: Challenges the validity of Stuart's statement.)

Stuart: Well, it could be!?

(2d: Some argumentative challenge is now taking place.)

Ben: I thought about the bit in the police station. He could have murdered someone, or something, and he was an eye-witness and they were questioning him to find out what he looks like. That's just an artist's impression.

(3d: Ben joins Alison, in attempting to construct a wider hypothesis, using the variety of pictorial evidence.)

Stuart: Well, that man is probably like a padre, or something like that. The church has been robbed and then the policeman goes to the laboratory and he asks where you were at the time.

(2f and 4b: Offers further supplementary statements to clarify his own position.)

Ben: She could be studying finger prints.

(5c: Ben validates Stuart's contribution.)

Stuart: And the carpenter has been fixing the shelves that have been smashed down in the robbery . . . I think this is something to do with that, because that's his church there, probably. . .

(2b: Clarifies own ideas.)

Teacher: You think that is something to do with that?
Stuart: Yes that is something to do with that and that is his church which has been robbed. And she's looking for finger prints. He's trying to put the shelves back together. He's going to help him. . . and the bottom one he's trying to find out what's wrong with the car.

(2j: Attempts to summarize the groups' ideas, so far.)

Ben: Is there any proof in the car? For instance, these jigsaw pieces, that could be in the east of the World, that could be in the north of the World, that could be in the south, and that could be in the west of the World.

(3b and 4c: Further evidence offered to support the main idea of the argument. Ben also uses some distinctive argumentative terminology, such as 'proof' and 'for instance').

Teacher: so each picture is to do with the points of the compass?

Ben: Yes. . . the south is at the bottom, on the left . . . and the same with the east, north and west. If you just sort of place that there, in the middle, the east will be that way the north that way and the west that way.

(3i: Ben summarizes his ideas, to the satisfaction of the others). The discussion proceeds with a new focus on the role of the policeman and whether, or not it is a scene from everyday life. This further discussion also requires limited teacher intervention and engages a rich variety of pupils through the STS approach.

Informal

a) *Children's remarks*
• *What are Somerset Thinking Skills about?*
'It's like detective work'
'looking for clues'
'something you have to look for to get evidence'

• *Do you enjoy Thinking Skills (TS) lessons?*
'Yes, I like finding out new things'
'I like using each others ideas'
'I like the puzzles, it gets your brain working'
'It makes us slow down and think so we don't make so many mistakes'
'We have to think, argue, discuss, use the evidence and give reasons'
'I think TS is brilliant, I told my dad all about it. I told him all these words we use and what they mean. He was really impressed. I think its really good the way we share our ideas and have to listen and sometimes bear with them even if we don't really agree'
'It's like politics, I want to be a politician when I'm older and this is really useful'
'I really like TS. I don't mind talking out now. No one laughs at me'
'I really feel I'm using my brain in TS, and I never get bored like in some lessons'
'I like disagreeing'
'I love the argument'

• *Examples of Transfer*

After a maths test, a boy commented, 'I worked out a strategy for doing that test, I did all the ones I could do first, then went back and thought more about the more difficult ones'.

What thinking skills do we use in real life? Examples of children's replies, follow:

Explaining: 'It's important to make sure everyone understands what they have to do. We need to explain where to go, give directions when someone asks'.

Classifying: 'You need to classify evidence e.g. put all the people wearing tartan trousers together, then you can eliminate the rest. In Science we have to classify groups too'.

Analysing and synthesizing: 'We need to pull things apart so we can put them back together, like when we did that lesson on the attack. A detective would need to do that too.'

Evaluating: 'You evaluate all the evidence and put it together to make a hypothesis. In this hypothesis you fit it all together in your mind, which is synthesizing. You create a cartoon in your head and see who actually did it, that's mentally visualizing, so you can put all the evidence together and see clearly in your own way.'

Comparing: 'You need to compare and check to see if you are right. If you were looking into an incident, you would have to compare the statements, put them together and create a scene so you can find out what people are lying and who did the crime.'

Recognizing implicit cues: 'Like when you scan a picture, then you find out information isn't in the information box, but it doesn't say it.'

Explicit instruction: 'An act of mental and physical ability.'

Eliminating: 'It's like a detective when he has five suspects. He can eliminate them by getting descriptions of them and compare it against each of them. If they don't fit he eliminates them.'

b) *Other teachers' remarks*

For example in Design and Technology, the teacher observed that:

I find it difficult to comment on the performance of the group during the autumn term. There was little to differentiate the group from the other two at that time.

It became clear in the spring term that they were more voluble, eager to progress, quick to answer, prepared to discuss problems without prompting. Difficulties were overcome by seeking and accepting advice from peers.

There was great co-operation. Advice and help were offered with very few derogatory remarks being made of each others work.

c) *Observations of STS lessons by other teachers*
For example HoD English who observed a number of lessons said:

> All children showed total involvement, hardly any signs of time wasting or failings in concentration.
>
> I was impressed with the language used by Gareth and Matthew in their various exchanges, questions and answers and the development of conversations which occurred. Gareth used the following in one exchange, 'grid, situation, proof, evidence, reference point'.
>
> The girls communicated well. The girl who first chose the treasure's hiding place appreciated the subtleties involved. I was impressed with the patience shown by the listeners in the whole group discussions, spontaneous comments were made, but didn't interfere with the flow of the discussion.

CONCLUDING REMARKS

The introduction of the Somerset Thinking Skills Modules into the curriculum of these 9–10 year old children has led to marked improvements in their oracy skills. The children's use of higher-order language skills and cognitive strategies, their social awareness, and attitudes to new work had all developed apace. They have learnt the value of enjoying argumentative discourse and appreciated some of its importance for the development of their own thinking.

ANNEX

A cognitive instrument, outlining developmental features of oral argument in the small group discussions of 7–11 year olds

1. Outline of idea(s) for argument:
a) Offers opinion, or point of view, with no explanation.
b) Offers an opinion, or egocentric point of view, with limited explanation.
c) Offers a general opinion (an assertion), with reasonable explanation.
d) Offers an assertion with some reasoning, but no supportive interpretation.
e) Offers an assertion, with some reasoning and reasonable interpretation.
f) Uses anecdote to illuminate an idea and support position.
g) Connects ideas into a basic hypothesis, with some abstract reasoning.
h) Offers a coherent hypothesis, supported by relevant information.

2. Clarifying of ideas:
a) Offers some explanation, when challenged.
b) Clarifies own ideas without challenge.
c) Recognizes irrelevancies in other contributions, by challenging others.
d) Challenges others to clarify their ideas, by questioning.
e) Proposes supplementary statement(s) to support own position, upon being challenged.
f) Proposes supplementary statement(s) to support own position, with challenge.
g) Clarifies others' points of view and ideas, without invitation (supportive or critical).
h) Called on as an 'expert' to assist others with their clarification.
i) Summarizes own ideas.
j) Summarizes group ideas.

3. Supporting with evidence:
a) Offers an acceptable reason(s) to support point of view.
b) Offers some evidence to support the main idea of the argument.
c) Requests evidence from other participants to support their views.
d) Uses evidence to construct an hypothesis.
e) Selects appropriate evidence to support an hypothesis.

4. Knowledge about argumentative language:
a) Some basic introductory language to introduce ideas (e.g. I think, in my opinion, I agree but).
b) Uses some tentative terms to allow speculative thinking (e.g. maybe, perhaps, possibly).
c) Uses distinct argumentative terminology (e.g. persuade, convince, argue).
d) Experiments with abstract terms and phrases, albeit without a clear understanding (i.e. trying-out adult argumentative terms e.g. thesis, hypothesis, rhetoric).

5. Appreciation of Ideas:
a) Egocentric commitment to own ideas (unaware and uninterested in alternative points of view).
b) Some limited appreciation of another contribution (indicated by active listening and non-verbal response).
c) Recognizes another point of view by offering a reasonable and relevant response (validating the contribution).
d) Evaluates a contribution by offering some further information.
e) Evaluates a contribution by critical reasoning.
f) Evaluates a contribution by offering an alternative hypothesis, building-on the contributions of others.

g) Appreciates and understands the importance of evidence to support a hypothesis and develop an argument.

REFERENCES

Blagg N, Ballinger, M and Gardner, R (1988) *Somerset Thinking Skills Course*, Oxford: Blackwell.
Feuerstein, R, Rand, Y and Hoffman, M B (1979) *The Dynamic Assessment of Retarded Performers*, Baltimore: University Park Press.
Rosenthal, K and Jacobson, L F (1968) *Pygmalion in the Classroom*, New York: Holt, Rinehart and Winston.
Tann, S (1990) 'Language skills and pupil needs; Oracy in the classroom' in Jones, N (ed) *Special Educational Needs Review* Vol. 3, Lewes: Falmer Press.
Wilkinson, A (1971) *The Foundation of Language, Talking and Reading in Young Children*, Oxford: Oxford University Press.

Chapter 10

Reading Recovery: It's not what you do it's the way you do it

Peter Geekie

INTRODUCTION

The fact that children can spend long periods in school without learning to read and write is a perennial problem for school systems throughout the world. All types of solutions have been tried, from withdrawal schemes based on behaviour modification strategies, to the use of whole language strategies by teachers working in the child's normal classroom. And while all approaches have been effective for some children, none can claim to have produced really substantial gains in reading performance for the majority of the children involved.

In the last decade, however, a programme which originated in New Zealand has been attracting international interest because it can support its claims of effectiveness by reference to a number of carefully conducted research studies. The programme is called Reading Recovery, and it has grown out of the work of Dr Marie Clay of Auckland University. Since 1984 Reading Recovery has been established successfully in parts of Australia and the United States. It is surprising, however, to find that the programme is not properly understood, even in the regions where its results are attracting widespread attention, so it seems sensible, as a starting point, to outline briefly the essential features of Reading Recovery.

What is Reading Recovery?

Marie Clay has written that when she was a clinical child psychologist who frequently came into contact with children experiencing difficulties in learning to read, she became '. . . tired of seeing long, long waiting lists which could not be cleared, of late referrals and admissions to special help, and of remedial programs that were minimally successful' (Clay, 1986, p. 2). It is not surprising, then, to find that the programme which she developed is designed to avoid those shortcomings. It seeks to offer early assistance to all children who seem to need it, and to help them to achieve at least average levels of attainment in their literacy skills. In more detail the critical features of the programme are as follows:

- Reading Recovery is not a remedial programme. It is a prevention programme aimed at cutting back the incidence of reading failure in the senior school.
- It is based on the early identification of 'at risk' readers. In New Zealand children identified by their teachers as being in the bottom half of their group are tested on their sixth birthday, exactly one year after they have entered formal education.
- Children are not excluded from the programme because of their social origins, ethnicity, school history, physical handicaps, or previous development.
- The children selected do not have to fall below any specified attainment level. Whatever the overall level of achievement at the school, the Reading Recovery children will be those at the bottom of the group in terms of their literacy development.
- Accelerated progress is expected. The objective is to raise the children's reading performance to at least an average level so that they can cope with the literacy demands of their usual classroom. It is only when children are judged to be functioning normally in their own classroom that they are discontinued from the programme.
- The children selected are given 30 minutes of intensive, responsive individual tuition daily by a specially trained Reading Recovery teacher for a period not exceeding 20 weeks. Children who have been in the programme for 20 weeks without showing the expected accelerated progress will be referred on for more highly specialized assistance.
- Reading Recovery teachers are junior school teachers who have had previous experience of teaching successful readers.
- The teachers receive their training in a year-long in-service course involving fortnightly group sessions run by trained tutors. During these sessions each participant takes a turn at teaching behind a one-way screen while the rest of the group watches and analyses his/her teaching. The tutors also engage in regular follow-up visits to the teachers in their own schools to discuss problems and offer advice and support.
- Teachers are involved in Reading Recovery sessions for at least two hours daily, but work in a normal classroom setting for the balance of the day. They should not be teachers in executive positions.
- The Reading Recovery teacher should not work in isolation but should be part of a team involving the whole school. A

close working relationship with the junior school teachers is especially important.

EVALUATING READING RECOVERY IN CENTRAL VICTORIA

Background to the trial

The Field Trial of Reading Recovery in Central Victoria took place in 1984. It was an entirely local initiative. For some years in-service courses on literacy had been offered to teachers in the region. Many of these courses had been presented by a team from the Riverina College of Advanced Education under the leadership of Dr Brian Cambourne. While these courses had contributed significantly to the development of a better understanding of literacy, teachers had found difficulty in translating theory into good classroom practice. Consequently, a continuing search had gone on for a programme that would not only help to minimize the number of children with reading difficulties in the local schools but also provide in-service education for teachers. The achievement of genuine change in teachers' knowledge and skills was seen to be just as important as improving the children's reading skills.

This search led to Reading Recovery, and it was decided that a Field Trial of the programme should be arranged. This was no small enterprise, especially since no specific assistance was offered by the Victorian Education Department. In order to introduce Reading Recovery to Central Victoria a way had to be found, in the absence of special funding, to have a local teacher trained as a Reading Recovery tutor in New Zealand. This problem was solved by obtaining an International Teaching Fellowship for the chosen teacher, who subsequently completed the course of training in 1983. When she returned to commence working on the implementation of the programme in Victoria she was accompanied by an experienced New Zealand tutor whose task it was to provide support and guidance during the implementation year.

The nature of the qualitative study

It was early in 1984, after the Field Trial had actually commenced, that two Senior Education Officers from Central Victoria came to the University of Wollongong to see if Dr Brian Cambourne and members of his Centre for the Study of Literacy, would be prepared to carry out a qualitative evaluation of the programme to complement the quantitative study which had already begun. Consequently, in April a qualitative evaluation of the Field Trial began. The basic intention of the evaluation was to promote a better understanding of the Field Trial by developing a complex and accurate account of it. In order to do this, data had to be collected which reflected the various perspectives of the groups involved in the Trial. The trustworthiness of the evaluators' summaries of the data was checked by reference to the participants themselves.

The information collected during the evaluation came mainly from observations and semi-structured interviews. It was primarily on the basis of observation that an understanding of the context of the Trial was developed. First-hand experience of the conditions under which teachers worked, and some feeling for the personal relationships between the participants, provided the basis for this understanding. Many of these observations were informal but the evaluators also observed a number of Reading Recovery lessons being conducted, and attended three in-service sessions.

The interviews were semi-structured, and were designed to allow the participants to talk freely about the things which concerned them most. The groups interviewed included the key administrators, the Reading Recovery tutors and teachers, the principals of the Reading Recovery schools, and selected groups of parents and non-Reading Recovery teachers. In all, 162 individual interviews were conducted yielding a series of verified accounts of what each of the groups believed to have happened during the Field Trial. The comments below are derived from those interviews, and are grouped under headings representing the issues that the participants themselves believed to be important.

WHAT THE INTERVIEWS TOLD US

The effects of the programme

Improvements in reading
All groups reported significant *growth in the reading performance* of the children. Both the tutors and the Reading Recovery teachers said that children had made accelerated progress, and had been discontinued from the programme. Data from other sources supported these claims (Smith, 1986). Most principals, for example, reported instances of children who had been expected to be slow learners but whose reading had reached at least an average standard because of their inclusion in the programme. The parents and the teachers from whose classes the children had been drawn also verified the progress made by the children. Many parents remarked on a noticeable growth of interest in reading as a leisure activity.

There were, of course, some children who had been in the programme for excessively long periods of time. The tutors attributed this to a number of causes:

- the inexperience of the teachers;
- the fact that some teachers had allowed their sympathies for the children to divert them from a single-minded concentration on teaching them to read; and
- the fact that some teachers had not realized what Reading Recovery really required them to do because they had been too assured of their own knowledge of how to teach reading.

Ten children of the 121 involved in the programme were considered to need more specialized assistance than Reading Recovery could offer, but overall the number of children who had not made the expected progress represented a very small percentage of the Grade One group from which they had been drawn. Also, not all the children had developed an increased interest in reading; there were some whose reading had improved greatly but who showed no greater interest in reading or other school activities.

Changes in the children's attitudes
The development of the children's *self-esteem and confidence* was almost always mentioned first, even before comments were made about the improvement in their reading skills. Growth in independence was also frequently mentioned as a positive effect of involvement in the programme. Instead of being defeated by difficulties, the children were now prepared to take chances. These behaviours were not restricted to the Reading Recovery sessions but were also observed in the usual classroom setting. Many children, who had previously been difficult in class were now well behaved and co-operative. These changes were also noticed in the home. Many parents commented that their children were happier and more confident because of the development of their reading ability.

Changes in the Reading Recovery teachers
The tutors stressed that Reading Recovery was not designed to promote teacher change. It was directed towards improving the children's reading, not changing teachers. Nevertheless, the trainee teachers themselves were conscious of the changes that had occurred in their *understanding of reading and learning in their teaching competence.* Some of the teachers were also aware of personal change as well as professional growth. They said that their new knowledge and skills had developed their self-esteem and confidence. School principals verified that these changes had taken place. They noted increased confidence and commitment in many of the teachers, and were generally impressed by their competence and effectiveness. The parents, too, unanimously approved of the teachers' efforts to help their children. They

frequently nominated the teacher's enthusiasm and skill as contributing most to the effectiveness of the programme.

Selection of teachers

The selection of teachers for training as Reading Recovery teachers in Central Victoria differed significantly from the ideal procedures suggested by the originators of the programme. Among those selected for training were a number who did not meet the usual criteria. For example, a number of teachers who were in executive positions were included, as were teachers with no junior school experience.

In the northern part of the region teachers attached to the Special Education Unit in that district were persuaded to undertake training as Reading Recovery teachers. These teachers not only had no experience in teaching reading to junior school children, but had also been given specialist training in methods of instruction which were radically different to those of Reading Recovery. Such teachers would never, under normal circumstances, have been selected for inclusion in the programme.

The administrators and tutors were fully conscious of the types of problems which seemed likely to occur because of the violation of the selection procedures, but they proceeded because waiting for more suitable circumstances would almost certainly have meant that the Field Trial would not have happened at all.

Resistance to Reading Recovery

Resistance to Reading Recovery came from a number of sources. The Victorian Education Department Curriculum Department, for example, expressed a range of reservations about the programme. Withdrawal of pupils was contrary to official policy and was seen to be very undesirable. Reservations were also expressed about the programme because it was seen to be item specific, and required mastery of all items of knowledge before the children were involved in actual reading and writing. Finally it was believed that the programme was cost-ineffective because it involved individual instruction instead of group instruction.

There had also been widespread scepticism about the programme in Central Victoria at the beginning of the year. There was some feeling that Reading Recovery was being promoted because of a temporary enthusiasm, and that it would soon be abandoned. The greatest scepticism and resistance came from the Upper School, where teachers often felt that an excessive proportion of the available resources was being used for the benefit of a small number of first grade children. Even among the Reading Recovery teachers themselves there was some scepticism. The

Special Education teachers, in particular, were not convinced, initially, that anything new was being offered.

During the year these signs of resistance diminished considerably. The entire group of Reading Recovery teachers had become obviously committed to the programme. The Special Education teachers became enthusiastic about the new perspective on learning that they had gained. And the reservations felt by many of the principals and other teachers were replaced by support for the programme. A growing level of interest throughout the region was also evident. Schools which had shown no interest in becoming involved at the beginning of 1984 now wished to have a teacher trained.

Resources

a) Although a genuine attempt was made to provide special allocations of funds for the purchase of books, in most cases obtaining an adequate supply of books was a problem for the teachers.

b) In most schools the teaching space provided for the Reading Recovery lessons was not suitable. Lessons were often held in places like store rooms and corridors.

Deficits in background knowledge and experience

One thing which made the early stages of the Field Trial more difficult was the fact that the Australian teachers did not have the same background of knowledge as the New Zealand counterparts. This meant that the initial screening of children for selection, and the testing of the entire group for research purposes created great difficulties because the Australian teachers were not familiar with the types of assessment which were commonly used in New Zealand.

Pressure

a) The most frequently mentioned source of anxiety for the Reading Recovery teachers was the in-service course. This anxiety was mainly associated with having to teach behind the one-way screen in front of their peers, but they also found the way in which their existing knowledge and beliefs were challenged very stressful.

b) The intensity of the individual sessions for two hours daily was also a source of pressure. All the trainees found teaching in the programme very demanding and much more tiring than ordinary classroom teaching.

c) The anxiety of trying to move children through the programme also troubled teachers. This anxiety was particularly intense when they had difficulty in discontinuing their first child.

d) The pressure of being on display before visitors and evaluators was also frequently mentioned during the interviews.
e) The teachers also felt that they were subjected to the pressure of 'making it work'. They felt that they had to justify the allocation of resources to the programme by the results they produced.
f) Their awareness of the negative reactions of some of their colleagues also created anxieties. Many of the teachers felt isolated in their schools because there was no one with whom they could share their problems and achievements.

Attitudes to learning and knowledge

The tutors said that in order to learn how children learn to read, the teachers first had to learn to observe accurately. Once this had been accomplished they were able to learn from the children, especially their most successful child. It was during the process of getting this child out of the programme that the Reading Recovery teachers became aware of the behaviours that characterize competent reading.

When they were asked to reflect on their experience in the in-service course, both the tutors and the teachers said that learning often involves discomfort. Most of the trainee Reading Recovery teachers said that, in order to make progress in learning about how children learn to read, they first had to have their existing beliefs shattered. This had been an extremely disturbing experience for them, but they had eventually recognized that some level of discomfort was probably inevitable if true learning was to take place.

On the other hand, when they spoke about their work with the children, the trainee teachers said that learning requires the development of an atmosphere of trust, and will only occur if instruction begins with what the children already know. It was stressed that there was no end point to learning. As expectations were gradually raised so would the individual continue to learn.

It was also said that something was not truly known until it had been articulated. It was not sufficient that the trainees should show their understanding in the way they taught. It was only when they could explain the behaviour of both teacher and child in the observed lessons, and defend their explanations in rational terms, that they could be said to have really learnt how children learn to read.

Objectivity

The tutors placed great emphasis on the objectivity of the judgements made about different aspects of the programme. The theory upon which it had been built was based on 'objective' observations of children reading. The 'objective' data derived from the Diagnostic Survey made the selection of children for inclusion in the programme more reliable, and served as a source of support for the teachers' intuitive judgements. Training in accurate observation made it possible for the Reading Recovery teachers to draw on 'objective' sources of information as a basis for their responses to children. As a result it was not likely that changes to the programme would be made.

Impact of Reading Recovery

All groups knew something about Reading Recovery. They knew that it was intended to give some children who had been experiencing difficulty another chance to learn to read properly. They knew that it involved passing through 'levels' and involved careful observations of the children's reading through 'running records', although they were not very sure what they were.

When they were asked about the most important features of the programme, the sessions of individual instruction were almost always mentioned first. Most people knew that the instruction sessions were highly structured and intensive, and that reading and writing were taught together. Some teachers said that it featured positive reinforcement, mastery of items of information, and the eradication of wrong responses.

Parents noted different things. They nominated the high quality of the teaching and the interest and enthusiasm of the teachers as the most important features. They also spoke of the appropriate choice of books which they said were far better than those normally used in schools.

Most of the principals and teachers also said that there seemed to be nothing especially novel about Reading Recovery. They referred to similarities between it and other remedial programmes they had encountered in their teaching careers. Reading Recovery was seen as a very effective, well structured and highly organized approach to teaching remedial reading.

Isolation and secrecy

Most of the Reading Recovery teachers felt some degree of isolation from the rest of the staff in their schools. At the beginning of the year very few local teachers knew anything about the programme. They had many questions they wished to ask. Unfortunately, the trainee teachers were advised not to answer questions until they knew more about the programme themselves. As a result many teachers throughout the region believed that there was a deliberate 'air of secrecy' about the programme. This had seriously troubled some of the Reading

Recovery teachers and increased the distance between them and their colleagues.

THE EVALUATORS' PERSPECTIVE ON THE FIELD TRIAL

The information in the previous section was drawn from comments made by the various groups of participants during the interviews. In this section the evaluators' comments on the Field Trial are presented. It needs to be stressed that these comments are not presented as a statement of the ultimate truth about the Field Trial.

Change

Although no attempt had been made by the evaluators to monitor changes in any formal way, it was inevitable that most of the informants would wish to talk about the various types of changes they had witnessed taking place during the Field Trial. Some of the changes they referred to are discussed below.

Changes in the level of support for Reading Recovery
Few teachers or principals knew anything about the programme when the Field Trial was first proposed. As a result, persuading schools to become involved was a problem. Eventually all schools which were prepared to be involved had been included. No selection process was involved. Also, the decision to become involved had sometimes been made by the principal alone, rather than in consultation with his teachers, and even in the schools which had volunteered to become involved, support was by no means unanimous. Many Upper School teachers at the beginning of the year had been unhappy about the diversion of resources into a programme that was designed to serve the needs of a small number of 6-year-old children. In order to make the Field Trial possible these teachers had suffered some loss of support in other curriculum areas. Under these circumstances some resentment of Reading Recovery was not surprising.

By the end of the year, however, most of the resistance among the Upper School teachers had disappeared. The schools involved in the Field Trial voted to continue in the programme and 12 more teachers from the State system and six from the Catholic system were to be trained as Reading Recovery teachers in 1985.

What this means is that experienced teachers across the grades had decided that the outcomes of the programme seemed to justify its continuation and expansion. This shift in attitude does not prove that Reading Recovery had achieved its objectives, but it does clearly demonstrate that the community of teachers in the region had been favourably impressed by the gains made, despite their initial scepticism.

The changes that occurred at the system level similarly indicate that the education community believed that the observable achievements of Reading Recovery justified further support. Two more teachers, one from each system, were to be sent to New Zealand to be trained as tutors. The Catholic Education Department had also decided that resources should be diverted from Special Education into Reading Recovery because it had been seen to produce better results. This practical commitment constitutes a declaration of confidence in the programme and support for its continuation by the administrators of both systems in Central Victoria.

Changes in confidence and independence
Other studies of Reading Recovery have focused on quantifiable aspects of reading performance. This evaluation, however, highlights the other changes that took place among the participating children. All the interviewed groups said that most of the children in the programme had shown increased independence and higher self-esteem. They obviously considered this to be at least as important as any growth in reading ability which they had observed. Not only had the children's behaviour improved, but they were also approaching their schoolwork across the curriculum with greater confidence. In this way the programme could be seen to have successfully attacked a basic cause of learning disability rather than just preventing the development of reading difficulties. This outcome of the programme, which is usually ignored, needs to be recognized as one of its most significant achievements.

The in-service course

The Reading Recovery in-service course was very successful in convincing most of its participants that they should alter long-held beliefs about teaching and learning, and that they should re-examine knowledge that seemed to be securely grounded in their own professional experience. Genuine change in these teachers was achieved and that makes it worthy of close examination, especially by other in-service educators.

Amongst the features of the course which seemed to contribute most to its effectiveness were:

- the regular fortnightly sessions over a full year;
- the requirement that each participant must teach in front of the others and have his/her teaching made the subject of discussion and analysis;

- the requirement that the teachers should be able to articulate their understandings and beliefs;
- the fact that the teachers involved in the course had to return to their schools and put into practice what they were learning; and
- the regular follow-up visits by the tutors to observe the teachers in action, and to give guidance and support.

But the feature of the course which was probably most significant was the fact that the teachers were trained to become accurate observers of children's learning behaviours. Once this was achieved they were able to check the usefulness of the knowledge they were acquiring against the reality of what children did in actual learning situations. In this way the trainees were moved towards becoming self-correcting teachers, just as they are expected to lead the children towards being self-correcting learners. This should be of special interest to anyone involved in teacher education at any level.

Effective learning
Because the usual criteria for selection had not been applied, a significant number of the people who were trained as Reading Recovery teachers in Central Victoria in 1984 held beliefs about teaching and learning which conflicted with those embodied in the programme. The Special Education teachers, in particular, found that their existing beliefs and skills were seriously challenged by the tutors, though most of the other teachers also felt that their previous experience and existing knowledge were not valued. In fact the stress which was experienced by most of them early in the year was caused by the aggressive way their beliefs and knowledge were challenged during the in-service sessions.

By the end of the year, however, they had developed a different perspective on their experience. They said that the early discomfort they had sufered had been an unavoidable and necessary stage in their personal learning process, and that some level of distress was necessary in order that serious self-examination might take place.

This did not match the attitude to learning which guided the teachers' behaviour in their contacts with the children. In the tuition sessions the emphasis was on using what the child already knew as the basis for learning; on building an atmosphere of trust between teacher and child; and on challenging the children without ever asking them to attempt tasks beyond their current capacity. This is as it ought to be, but it highlights an inconsistency which needs to be resolved. On the one hand the children's learning was said to have proceeded most efficiently when stress levels were low; on the other, stress was said to be a prerequisite to learning for the adults. If we assume, quite reasonably, that the conditions which contribute to effective learning must be the same whether children or adults are involved, then the claim that teachers need to have their existing knowledge and beliefs aggressively challenged and destroyed before they can develop a fresh perspective on teaching and learning should not be accepted uncritically. Instead, an effort should be made to discover whether a gentler approach to the in-service sessions might not work equally well. It might not be possible to remove all sources of anxiety from the in-service sessions, but it should be possible to avoid undervaluing the teachers' existing knowledge, and to challenge them without pushing them beyond their current capacities.

The development of commitment

It was said that commitment to Reading Recovery took hold when trainee teachers started to see children moving successfully through the programme, but it is important to recognize that the teachers did not begin to see results immediately. They were, after all, in the process of learning themselves and during the early months of training, most of them reached a stage of high anxiety and frustration when they had difficulty getting their first child out of the programme. Under other circumstances many teachers would almost certainly have abandoned what they were doing and assumed that the programme had not worked, but because these teachers had undertaken to be in the programme for a full year, and had the support of the tutors and the other trainee teachers, they persisted. Once the first child was discontinued, their belief in the effectiveness grew rapidly. And with each child their confidence in the programme grew. The simple lessons, that people become committed to what seems to be effective, and that persistence is needed to make something succeed, should not be missed.

Perhaps even more important is what the growth in commitment in the teachers tells us about the reality of the children's reading development. Like all the other groups involved, the trainee Reading Recovery teachers knew little about the programme at the beginning of the year, and certainly showed no special commitment to it. Their attitudes ranged from indifference to open scepticism. But when the interviews were conducted in November, the whole group showed a high level of commitment to the programme and defended its principles and practices. These changes occurred because they could point to the children who had entered the programme with minimal reading skills but were now functioning competently as readers and writers in their classrooms. Statistics showing the numbers of children discontinued from the programme are interesting, but they are not nearly as convincing as the conviction and commitment displayed by experienced teachers giving details of the children who had returned to their classrooms as effective readers. The change from indifference to enthusiasm in these teachers, created by the outcomes of their own teaching, is convincing evidence that the gains being made were genuine and significant.

Communicating about the programme

It was often said by the tutors and the trainee teachers that the only way to understand Reading Recovery properly was to teach in the programme and such a statement reflects the exclusiveness which seemed to be characteristic of the programme, at least as it was operating during the 1984 Field Trial. One of the consequences of this attitude was an adverse influence on some aspects of communication. Even the Reading Recovery teachers themselves felt that the flow of information was seriously restricted at the beginning of the year, indicated by the fact that other groups knew very little about the programme except for the most superficial details. Better communication about the objectives, principles and practices of Reading Recovery would have meant that there was less misunderstanding of it, and that other teachers might have been led to understand that it was not the packaging and organization of old 'methods' that characterized Reading Recovery, but a distinctive orientation to teaching.

Better communication with parents might also have enhanced the effectiveness of the programme. It was true that Reading Recovery, in many cases, improved the quality of contact between parents and schools, and between parents and their children; but still more might have been done because it was clear that at least some parents did not properly understand what was expected of them when the children brought their 'cut-up sentence' home from school each day. In fact, it seems that contacts with parents should be a focus for Reading Recovery in the future, because the full potential of such contacts is not being realized.

Resistance to change

It was often said that the programme had been derived 'objectively' from research, and had been justified 'objectively' in trials. It is obvious that such appeals to the authority of 'objective facts' are based on a narrow view of what counts as knowledge, and this is important in understanding why the programme is so resistant to any suggestions of possible change.

It is reasonable to expect that any programme should be properly established before any changes are considered. And it is understandable that the organizers and controllers of Reading Recovery should resist suggestions of change from people who do not display a full understanding of its true nature and intentions.

What is disturbing is that most people involved in Reading Recovery clearly believe that improvements are inconceivable. It is possible that Reading Recovery is the ultimate solution to the problem of illiteracy in our schools, but it is more likely that it will develop in positive directions in the future if it includes a process of constant critical review of its practices, and if it makes continuing efforts to keep its tutors and teachers aware of developments in literacy research and instruction. It might also be wise to reflect on the fact that not all knowledge is derived from the use of 'objective' methods of enquiry. In particular, there should be an acceptance of the validity of the intuitive insights of the experienced teachers selected for training in the programme. The Reading Recovery teachers interviewed in this study seemed to accept, without any reservations, the view of learning and literacy presented to them. It would be healthier to find a more questioning attitude amongst these teachers; quality controls are reasonable and necessary. Total resistance to change, however, is likely in the long term to have a negative effect on the future development of what is, in other respects, a very effective programme.

The impact of the programme on the teachers

Some aspects of the impact of Reading Recovery on the participating teachers have already been mentioned. But two other comments need to be made as well.

First, it was clear that the programme not only had a positive effect on the attitudes of the children but also boosted the self-esteem and confidence of some of teachers as well. Although the tutors stressed that such outcomes were of no real interest because the objective was simply to accelerate the reading development of the children, some principals and parents pointed to very noticeable changes for the better in some of the teachers involved. These changes, like the others cited earlier, are clear indications that the programme was far from neutral in its impact.

The second point is related to what the teachers said they had learnt from their involvement in the programme. Rather than just saying that they had learnt how to be more effective in their teaching of reading, they all said that they had learnt about how children learn. They went on to stress the collaborative nature of learning; they had come to believe that their role was not so much to direct and control the children's learning, but to help them to learn for themselves. The teachers' role was to observe accurately what the children were doing and then to respond sensitively and appropriately so that the children's attempts to learn were guided and sustained. The teachers are not just facilitators – they play an active part in promoting learning – but they also accept that ultimate responsibility for learning lies with the child. The child

·has to learn with the teacher, rather than being taught by them. In particular teachers are expected to employ astute questioning designed to help the children solve their own problems. The objective is not just to produce children who can respond to print, but to develop self-correcting, self-regulated learners. It is this orientation to teaching and learning which is at the heart of Reading Recovery, and it is the acceptance of it by the teachers it trains that is amongst its most significant achievements.

The cost-effectiveness of the programme

The question of cost-effectiveness frequently arose. It is not a question that can be conclusively answered. More research will not help. The nature of academic research is that it promotes debate, rather than providing answers. It seems that it might be best, under the circumstances, to pay more attention to the pragmatic judgements of teachers, principals and educational administrators who have had personal experience of Reading Recovery. These people cannot wait for data to accumulate. In the course of their daily work they make judgements and comparisons about programmes. They do this by drawing on their prior experience of children and teaching practices, and their observations of the successes and difficulties of programmes in action.

In Central Victoria at the end of 1984 it was these people who chose to support Reading Recovery, and in doing so they made a clear judgement that it was more effective than other available ways of trying to achieve universal literacy. Since 1984 other educators in other regions of Australia have made similar judgements. Reading Recover has become firmly established throughout Victoria and in the Australian Capital Territory, and is now being introduced into New South Wales. This does not prove the cost-effectiveness of the programme, but it does show that many educators at all levels believe that it is the most efficient way to minimize the number of children experiencing reading difficulties in their schools. Their judgements must be given the emphasis they deserve when the question of cost-effectiveness is raised.

CONCLUSION

It would normally be expected that an evaluation study of a reading programme would report on any changes in measured reading performance which could be attributed to it. Such information is always of great interest to anyone attempting to assess the effectiveness of a programme. But quantitative methods of evaluation leave out many of the most important indicators of the success or failure of a programme because they cannot be measured reliably. For example, during the Central Victorian Field

Trial of Reading Recovery, initial scepticism about the programme was transformed into support because it was seen to be bringing about a genuine acceleration in the children's reading ability. This growth in commitment would be difficult to quantify, but it is nevertheless one of the most persuasive sources of evidence that Reading Recovery is an effective way of preventing the growth of reading difficulties in young children. It is also an indication that the growth in reading skills which was said to have occurred was genuine. If experienced teachers and principals believe that the growth in reading skills they saw in the children was real and substantial, it seems reasonable to believe that this was the case.

The allocation of resources is always an indication of the true priorities of an education system. Consequently, the decision made by both the State and Catholic school systems to train additional tutors in New Zealand during 1985 is significant. It shows that the key administrators in the region were giving expansion of Reading Recovery a high priority. It shows that the programme was seen to have produced results which justified continued support from both education systems. The fact that it has now become a normal part of the Victorian education system, and has been established in parts of the United States and other parts of Australia demonstrates that confidence in its effectiveness has continued to grow. It seems self-evident that a programme which has attracted the interest and support of experienced educators in both Australasia and North America deserves close attention from any educational system seeking to ensure that all children reach secondary school able to read and write.

This does not mean that the evaluation offers an unqualified endorsement of the programme. While it seems likely that Reading Recovery is the best presently available approach to preventing the development of literacy difficulties, that should not be taken to mean that positive changes to the programme in the future are inconceivable. It was the resistance to change expressed by tutors and teachers during the Victorian Field Trial of Reading Recovery which was its most worrying feature. Like all programmes, it needs to subject its principles, practices and results to continuous critical scrutiny. Even if those who are involved have no doubts about any aspect of it, they should nevertheless develop the habit of systematically questioning its effectiveness.

For example, while they might feel justifiably proud of their successes in teaching children to read, they should not ignore the fact that it does not succeed with all children. It is not sufficient to claim that those who do not progress satisfactorily are special cases who need more specialized attention than Reading Recovery can offer. It would seem much more productive to investigate thoroughly why an approach that succeeds with so many, fails with a few. And in doing this it would seem sensible to use the observations and intuitions of the experienced and skilled teachers working within the programme as a primary source of data. Two other questions that might be asked of the programme immediately are whether the right children are always selected for tuition, and whether the methods of instruction used in the in-service course need modification.

These comments should not be taken to imply that Reading Recovery is necessarily flawed in the areas mentioned. It might be true that it cannot be improved. Perhaps no change will ever be necessary. What is important is that the people involved should not assume that no problems exist. The tutors and teachers should regularly raise questions about the programme, not because they doubt its effectiveness, but because complacency dulls awareness. If a deliberate, systematic effort is made to examine all aspects of the programme, it is much more likely to adapt to specific contextual circumstances, and to incorporate new knowlege so that it is always in a healthy state of growth.

It is also important that the true nature of the programme should be communicated accurately to those who are not directly involved. Too many people believed the essence of Reading Recovery was to be found in its organizational structures. The Reading Recovery teachers themselves knew better. They said that its key feature was the quality of their interaction with the children. They had learnt that learning is collaborative in nature. Their ultimate objective was not just to produce readers, but self-correcting, self-regulating learners. The truly distinctive feature of Reading Recovery is this orientation to teaching, not the way the programme is organized. If that is understood then misguided attempts to make it more cost-effective by using it with groups, rather than individuals, will not arise.

Finally, it needs to be said that literacy problems cannot be solved simply by teaching children to read and write. Obviously a mastery of the basic skills is necessary to achieve educational success, but it is not sufficient in itself. It is generally acknowledged that there is not one literacy, but many. Different cultures, and even different socio-economic groups within a single culture, use literacy in different ways and have differing attitudes to what it means to be literate. Our educational institutions, however, require that children should not just be able to read and write, but that they should think and communicate in ways that are specific to a certain type of literacy. Children who come from families, and attend schools, where these ways of speaking and writing and thinking are usual, and where exposure to the printed texts valued by the schooled community is unexceptional, have a distinct advantage. Such children find it much easier to satisfy the standards set by schools because the literacy they are developing is more like that of their teachers.

There is a literate culture that most schools take for granted and reward, but few teachers seem to have an explicit awareness of the nature of that culture or its importance. They focus on the development of 'skills' and on checking the children's 'comprehension'. In doing this they take time that would be much better spent in expanding the children's enjoyment of literature; in developing their familiarity with literate ways of saying things; and trying to use written language for reflection rather than simple communication. Every education system should strive to teach all children to read and write, and Reading Recovery might help them to achieve that objective. But now seems to be an appropriate time to shift away from debates about the methodology of basic literacy instruction, to how we might best meet the challenge of giving them full access to the culture of literacy.

REFERENCES

Clay, M C (1979) *Reading: The Patterning of Complex Behaviour*, 2nd Edn, Auckland: Heinemann Educational Books.

Clay, M C (1979) *The Early Detection of Reading Difficulties: A Diagnostic Survey with Recovery Procedures*, Auckland: Heinemann Educational Books.

Clay, M C (1982) *Observing Young Readers: Selected Papers*, Auckland: Heinemann Educational Books.

Clay, M C (1986) 'Why Reading Recovery Is The Way It Is', Unpublished manuscript.

Geekie, P C (1988) *Evaluation Report on the Reading Recovery Field Trial in Central Victoria, 1984*, University of Wollongong: Centre for Studies in Literacy.

Guba, E G and Lincoln, Y S (1982) *Effective Evaluation*, San Francisco: Jossey-Bass.

Lincoln, Y S and Guba, E G (1985) *Naturalistic Enquiry*, Beverley Hills: Sage Publications.

Smith, J (1986) 'Reading Recovery Report: March 1986', Unpublished manuscript.

Recommended Reading

Cohen, L. and Cohen, A. (1987) *Disruptive Behaviour: A Source Book for Teachers*, London Harper and Row/Paul Chapman.

Docking, J.W. (1987) *Control and Discipline in Schools: Perspective and Approaches* (2nd edition), London: Harper and Row/Paul Chapman

Watkins, C. and Wagner, P. (1987) *School Discipline: A Whole-school Approach*, Oxford: Blackwell.

Booth, T. and Coulby, D. (1987) *Producing and Reducing Disaffection*, Buckingham: Open University Press.

Morgan, D. and Hart, S. (1989) Improving Classroom Behaviour: New Directions for Teachers and Pupils, Cassell: London.

Jones, N. (1989) *School Management and Pupil Behaviour*, Lewes: Falmer Press.

Department of Education and Science (1989) *Discipline in Schools* (The Elton Report), London: HMSO.

Besag, V. (1989) *Bullies and Victims in Schools*, Buckingham: Open University Press.

Munn, P., Johnstone, M. and Chalmers, V. (1992) *Effective Discipline in Primary Schools and Classrooms*, London: Paul Chapman.

Munn, P., Johnstone, M. and Chalmers, V. (1992) *Effective Discipline in Secondary Schools and Classrooms*, London: Paul Chapman.

◆

REFERENCES FOR INTRODUCTION (from page 14)

Department of Education and Science (1987) *Education Observed 5: Good Behavior and Discipline in Schools*, London: DES.

Department of Education and Science (1989) *Discipline in Schools: HMI Working Group*, DES: HMSO.

Index